D0931509

**The Slow Speech
Development
of a Bright Child**

The Slow Speech Development of a Bright Child

Thelma E. Weeks
Center for Cross-
Cultural Research

Lexington Books

D.C. Heath and Company
Lexington, Massachusetts
Toronto   London

Library of Congress Cataloging in Publication Data

Weeks, Thelma E

The slow speech development of a bright child.

    1. Children—Language. 2. Gifted children. I. Title.
P136.W4   401'.9   73-23019
ISBN 0-669-91876-8

Copyright © 1974 by D.C. Heath and Company

All rights reserved. No part of this publication may be reproduced or transmitted in any form or by any means, electronic or mechanical, including photocopy, recording, or any information storage or retrieval system, without permission in writing from the publishers.

Published simultaneously in Canada.

Printed in the United States of America.

International Standard Book Number: 0-669-91876-8

Library of Congress Catalog Card Number: 73-23019

To Leslie

B&T   12.15   7.1.76

79414

Table of Contents

List of Figures

List of Tables

Preface

The research for this study covered a period of more than five years. Most recent child language acquisition studies have been of much shorter duration and have concerned a small group of children rather than just one child. I was much aware of this lack of recent longitudinal studies as I looked for other children to compare Leslie to at various ages. Also, a disproportionately large percentage of the children in other studies are first-born children, whose speech patterns seem to be somewhat different than those of the other children in the family. I hope this study will help to fill the gap I found.

The undertaking has been an unusually pleasurable one. Who could hope for a nicer research task than watching a two-month-old baby girl grow into a beautiful and charming little six-year-old girl? On her sixth birthday, Leslie asked me, "What do you want better—me or a thousand dollars?" A thousand dollars, indeed! She's priceless. And my experience in working with her has been priceless. I can only hope that my reporting of portions of it here will prove to be of value to the reader, also.

This study is based on research for my Stanford University doctoral dissertation. I am especially grateful to Professor Charles A. Ferguson, who encouraged me throughout the course of this research. His suggestions and constructive criticism have been invaluable. I also wish to thank Professors Susan Ervin-Tripp and Robert L. Politzer for their generosity in giving their time and thought to the research, and for their many helpful suggestions. Thanks are also due to Professor Robert C. Calfee for his insightful suggestions and to Professor Edith M. Dowley for her valued help in testing Leslie and commenting on the manuscript.

My deepest gratitide goes to Leslie, who was an active helper throughout the course of the study. I believe that her efforts in behalf of the research have been rewarding to her and I hope that subsequently they will benefit other children as well.

I especially want to thank Leslie's family, and Fred in particular, for their extensive help and cooperation. Thanks also go to John, Gregory, and Jennifer and their family for their cooperation.

Finally, I wish to thank my husband, Robert L. Weeks, for his patience and constant encouragement, without which I could never have completed the study.

Rationale for Phonetic Transcription

The objectives of this study were comparatively broad in scope—many aspects of Leslie's speech development were looked at, but none in minute detail. Therefore, it was not deemed desirable to make a narrow phonetic transcription of Leslie's speech. Many of her phonetic deviations from adult standards have been ignored, except where the inclusion serves some explanatory purpose, such as in Chapter 4 on phonological development. The usual goal was to make the transcription as readable as possible.

Rather than use the phonetic symbols more traditionally used by linguists, a greatly simplified set of notations has been devised for use here. The only variation in vowel sounds noted here will be between what has traditionally called "short and long" vowels. The short vowels (*e* as in p*e*t) are most frequently found, and can be thought of as the 'unmarked' member of the short/long pair. They will be indicated by a lower case letter. The long vowels (*E* as in b*ee*t) are less frequently heard and will be marked by capitalization for our purposes.

Only three diphthongs were deemed necessary to record Leslie's speech: *au* as in *out*, *Oi* as in *boy*, and *aw* as in *saw*.

We have not found it necessary to deviate from standard English orthography for the consonants, with the exception of noting the distinction between the voiceless dental fricative *th* (as in *thin*) and the voiced dental fricative *th* (as in *there*), and using *zh* for the sound of *z* in *azure*. Consonant combinations, such as *sh* for the initial sound of *she* and *ch* for the initial sound of *cheese* will also be used, as in standard orthography.

Phonetic Symbols and Other Notation
Used in Transcription

a	p*a*t	2;5	two years and five months of age
A	l*a*te	/ /	phonemic transcription
e	p*e*t	' '	gloss of phonemic material
E	b*ee*t	xxx	muttered or garbled utterance
i	b*i*t	V	vowel
I	b*i*te	C	consonant
o	n*o*t	+	a word boundary—the slight pause between two words
O	n*o*te		
u	p*u*tt	~	in free variation with
U	r*u*le, b*oo*k	$\begin{Bmatrix} E \\ \phi \end{Bmatrix}$	either item within the brackets may be selected
ə	*a*void, c*o*llect (the unstressed vowel)	→	read 'is written'
Oi	b*oy*	:	lengthening of the vowel
au	*ou*t		
aw	s*aw*		
th	*th*in		
th	*th*ere		
zh	a*z*ure		
?	glottal stop (as in ?Oh ?Oh)		

**The Slow Speech
Development
of a Bright Child**

1 Objectives

An often quoted reference to the ease and speed with which children acquire their first language is from Chomsky and Miller:

> How an untutored child can so quickly attain full mastery of a language poses a challenging problem for learning theorists. With diligence, of course, an intelligent adult can use a traditional grammar and a dictionary to develop some degree of mastery of a new language; but a young child gains perfect mastery with incomparably greater ease and without any explicit instruction. Careful instruction and precise programming of reinforcement contingencies do not seem necessary. Mere exposure for a remarkably short period is apparently all that is required for a normal child to develop the competence of a native speaker.[1]

Another oversimplification of the process of language acquisition is found in McNeil:

> The fundamental problem to which we address ourselves is the simple fact that language acquisition occurs in a surprisingly short time. Grammatical speech does not begin before one-and-one half years of age; yet, as far as we can tell, the basic process is complete by three-and-one-half years. Thus a basis for the rich and intricate competence of adult grammer must emerge in the short span of twenty-four months.[2]

Admittedly, some children do appear to acquire their first language quickly and effortlessly, but this is not true of all children. There is a wide variation in the learning pace of normal children. Jakobson noted this many years ago, and it remains true:

> While the succession of phonological acquisitions in child language appears to be stable in its fundamental characteristics, the speed of this succession is, in contrast, exceedingly variable and individual, and two "newly added phenomena" which directly succeed each other in one child can in another child be separated by many months, and even by years. There are children who

1

acquire the sound system of their native language especially quickly
and who are in full possession of it by about the middle of their
second year, while others still have not completely mastered their
phonemic system at school age.[3]

Fraser is one of those who have challenged Chomsky's assertions regarding
the speed and ease of language acquisition.[4] He maintains that the period for
the acquisition of syntax varies in approximately the same way and for the
same length of time that Jakobson says the phonological system varies. He
asks, "Is it so astonishing, if one is convinced that, for five or more years, the
child is working very hard and for long hours on mastering language? After all,
what else is there for a young child to do with his time! I think recent research
has demonstrated that some children, at least, do tackle the job most assiduously."
      Leslie, the bright child whose speech development this study is concerned
with, is one of those children who worked assiduously at the task of learning her
language. Her brother Fred, on the other hand, is one of those children referred
to by Chomsky and Miller who mastered his language with speed and apparent
ease.
      This study will look at the speech development of Leslie from the age of
two months to five years with the aim of examining how she is different in
language acquisition from children who acquire their language more rapidly,
and also with the hope of explaining certain aspects of how and why children
differ in their learning of language.
      This study will be, first of all, descriptive. There appears to be a need for
this, as we have found no other comprehensive studies of the language development of children whose speech development was slow but not pathological in
any apparent way. Researchers who have made detailed analyses of the syntactical development of young children have generally used subjects who were
easy to understand. This was a specific requirement in the selection of Adam,
Eve, and Sarah, for example, who have been studied over a period of several
years by Roger Brown and his associates at Harvard.[5] It is not yet known
whether or not there is a relationship between phonological development and
other aspects of language development, but if there is a positive relationship,
children who are slow in speech development have been automatically excluded
from most studies.
      We are not convinced that Leslie's pattern of speech development is more
unusual than Fred's, but it has been less studied. One reason for this is the
system of selection mentioned above. Most other children selected for study
are the children of linguists. Since linguists may be among those who learn
languages easily, it may be that their children will be among the fast language
learners, too.
      A second objective of this study will be to compare Leslie's speech develop-
ment with that of other children with the hope of finding patterns, such as

whether or not slow phonological development appears to correlate with slow syntactic development, and discovering what are some of the characteristics of phonological, syntactical, semantic, or paralinguistic development that slow speech developers share. Many patterns of language acquisition have been noted in the literature. Slobin comments, "Almost all investigators report a two-word (or two-morpheme) stage development. During this period the child can typically express such relations as agent-verb, verb-object, and agent-object, but cannot unite all three terms into a single utterance."[6] Again, Slobin states as a language universal: "The standard order of functor morphemes in the input language is preserved in child speech. . . . The elements of the English auxiliary phrase always occur in their proper order (e.g., 'has not been reading,' 'will not be able to come,' etc.)." Would a child who is slow in speech development follow these same patterns, but at a slower pace, or would there be qualitative differences other than those expected merely because of age differences, such as those noted between Sarah and Eve and Adam in Brown, Cazden and Bellugi-Klima?[7] Are there speech characteristics that can be considered as either predictors or indicators of slow speech development?

Throughout this study, Leslie's speech development will be compared with that of the children in Leopold,[8] Brown et al.,[9] and Bloom.[10] In some instances it will be compared with her brother Fred and her cousins John, Gregory, and Jennifer. In most chapters her speech development will also be compared with that of certain other children, and where appropriate, as with the Webster and Ingram study,[11] reports will be given of her performance on the same tests as those given to the children in the study being compared.

The third objective will be to look for causal factors for the slowness of Leslie's speech development. As Carroll points out, "There are large individual differences among adults in fluency of speaking performance, and there is evidence that suggests that these individual differences have their origin in early childhood and persist to a large extent throughout the pre-adult period."[12] Is there evidence that Leslie will "catch up" or does it appear that the child who develops slowly in speech production will be a non-fluent adult speaker?

Learning modalities (Birch and Belmont,[13] Goodnow,[14,15] Kendall[16]) suggest themselves as likely causative factors for slow speech development in children since it would seem that the mode of learning a first language is universally auditory except for deaf children who learn sign language. As Slobin points out:

> To a great extent, the form of linguistic rules is determined by the short-term processing limitations, because the rules refer to a system which is represented in the auditory-acoustic modality, and because they must be called into play during rapid speech processing. In fact, at the beginning levels, it could be that there is little difference between short-term processing strategies and linguistic rules.[17]

We may conclude, then, that if a child learns optimally by visual means rather than by the auditory mode, he will be disadvantaged in the task of language learning.

A recent theory of language learning proposed by Hebb, Lambert, and Tucker will also be examined to see if it might be explanatory in Leslie's case.[18],[19] They suggest that there are three kinds of learning involved in language acquisition. Two are kinds of latent learning (learning in which a person makes no apparent response at the time the learning occurs). These are perceptual learning and an association of ideas, or a sensory preconditioning (sometimes referred to as sensory-sensory association). The third kind of learning is a transient one-trial learning without reinforcement, which they call acquisition of information. These authors suggest that such elements in the language as plural morphemes are acquired in part by visual stimuli: a child sees one finger and he learns to say *finger*, when two fingers are held up, he learns to add /z/. They also explain that a child learns to say *doggie* on sight of a dog through a combination of sensory-sensory and perceptual learning, that is, visual-perception learning from the sight of dogs or similar objects, plus auditory-perceptual learning through repeated hearing of *doggie*.

The explanation of Hebb et al. of the acquisition of "nounness" involves the same learning modalities:

> In the first stage of language mastery, the child would notice the repeated coincidence of the mother's vocalizations with the appearance of attention-getting activity or a striking or noticeable object—a space-occupying, perceptible and imageable thing. Brown observes that the first nouns that a child masters refer to "concrete, tangible objects," and that the first verbs refer to "observable physical actions." Many neurons are excited when the mother draws a child's attention to some object and at the same time makes a particular sound. Different groupings of neurons are involved from one such occasion to the next, but the same sound will excite the same small sub-group on every occasion, and the organized activity of this sub-group becomes the abstract idea of a name. In this situation, then, the child perceives a particular word (lower-order cognition) but also perceives it as a name (higher-order, abstract activity accompanying the lower order). In the same way, the child learns to perceive action words as such.[20]

Slobin suggests "that human language is produced and received in rapid temporal sequence. That is to say, because we communicate through the rapidly-fading, temporally-ordered auditory modality, we must have strategies for quickly programming and deciphering messages. . . . The constraints on linguistic performance are both short-term and long-term. The short-term have to do with the ongoing use of speech, and the long-term with the storage and organization of the linquistic system."[21] The importance of the auditory modality in learning language cannot be questioned, but when a child has difficulties with this learning modality, it is of interest to know just which aspects of language learning are most apt to be affected by it. In Leslie's case, for example, we see that productive lexicon building appears to be inhibited more than other aspects of her language development. It is in this regard that the theory of Hebb et al. is explanatory. A great part of lexicon building, all except the most frequently used words, would fall into their third kind of learning—the acquisition of information. Leslie's active lexicon began to build rapidly after she began learning to read; the task had been converted, in part at least, from an auditory one to a visual one.

Another theory we wish to examine is Ervin-Tripp's.[22] She suggests that the Language Acquisition System (LAS) of a child is minimally comprised of the following five components:

1. Selective retention of features in short-term memory, particulary including order of acoustic input.
2. Phonological and semantic selection and reorganization for retention in long-term memory.
3. Interpretation templates, providing interpretations of structures according to the formal and semantic properties of sequences.
4. Successive processing by alternative heuristics, allowing shortcuts for frequent phrases, instances where non-linguistic determinants are strong, and so on.
5. Formal feature generation, identifying abstract classes and providing marking of the lexicon.

While the LAS of any child will consist of no less than these five components, it can easily be imagined that different children's capabilities in each of these areas might be very different. If, for example, Leslie's LAS were less proficient at performing the skills described by components numbered 1 and 5, and more proficient at performing skills described in 2, 3, and 4 than some other children, this might explain some differences in speech development. It is apparent in Leslie's case that she selects from what she hears and reorganizes it for retention in long-term memory, because she has learned a great deal by the age of five, and she had learned a great part of it auditorily. However, as will be seen from later discussions, she displays difficulty in short-term retention, particularly regarding the order of acoustic input. This way of viewing the problem may be more illuminating for the consideration of the development of a child's linguistic system than focusing on learning modalities, though learning modalities would seem to play a role in determining the level of functional efficiency of the various LAS components for any given child.

The final objective of the study will be to examine the educational implications of the research. If predictors of slow speech development can be found, is there a course of action that might be suggested to change the course of the speech development, such as tuition of one kind or another (Cazden,[23] Carroll,[24] John[25])? Or are there ways to help the child adapt to his slowness? What strategies does such a child use as a means of self-help, following an awareness of the difficulties?

Carroll, in pointing out that some people have considerable difficulty in learning foreign languages, says "Some people seem to have special difficulties in learning to remember the sounds and words of a foreign language; some people (not always the same ones) have special difficulties in learning the grammatical features."[26] Can predictions be made at early stages of child language acquisition as to whether or not that individual will learn a second language easily, or will learn certain aspects of it easily?

It appears that a lack of language fluency may affect school success negatively because teachers tend to judge children on such speech qualities as speed, pitch and intonation (Seligman, Tucker, and Lambert[27]). It may also affect job success, as reported by Hendrickson,[28] who asked a panel of professional people, judged to be urban liberals, non-prejudiced regarding race, to judge some Mexican-American junior high students according to whether or not they would consider them good potential employees (not necessarily for themselves). Judgments were made on the basis of video tapes. The panel selected the students who were most fluent—spoke rapidly and with confidence (rather than those with the least Spanish accent, as might have been expected).

Does slow speech development (an early lack of fluency) lead to a lack of language fluency in adulthood? If so, can anything be done about it?

The concentration of this study will be on individual differences as opposed to universals of language acquisition. Slobin says, "The problem of individual differences between children in their approaches to language acquisition has not been addressed frequently in developmental psycholinguistics, but is obviously of great importance—especially in light of the typically small samples required by longitudinal research methods."[29] This is the area in which it is hoped this study will make its principal contribution; however, ways in which Leslie's speech development does or does not follow universal patterns will be pointed out.

This study is not concerned with language-specific acquisition problems.

Notes

1. Noam Chomsky, and George A. Miller, "Introduction to the formal analysis of natural languages," in *Handbook of Mathematical Psychology*, vol. 2, edited by R. Luce, R. Bush and E. Galanter (New York: Wiley, 1963), pp. 275-76.
2. David McNeill, "Developmental psycholinguistics," in *The genesis of*

language, edited by Frank Smith and George A. Miller (Cambridge, Mass.: M.I.T. Press, 1966), p. 15.

3. Roman Jakobson, *Child language aphasia and phonological universals* (The Hague: Mouton, 1968; this paper first appeared in 1941), p. 46.

4. C. Fraser, "Discussion of the creation of language," in *Psycholinguistic papers,* edited by J. Lyons and R.J. Wales (Edinburgh: University Press, 1966), pp. 116-17.

5. Ursula Bellugi, "The acquisition of negation," Ph.D. dissertation, Harvard University, 1967, p. 3.

6. Dan I. Slobin, "Cognitive prerequisites for the development of grammar," in *Studies of child language development,* edited by C. A. Ferguson and Dan I. Slobin (New York: Holt, Rinehart and Winston, 1973), p. 195.

7. Roger Brown, Courtney Cazden, and Ursula Bellugi-Klima, "The child's grammar from I to III," in *Minnesota Symposia on Child Psychology,* vol. 2, edited by J.P. Hill (Minneapolis: University of Minnesota Press, 1968), pp. 28-73.

8. Werner F. Leopold, *Speech development of a bilingual child,* 4 vols (Evanston, Ill.: Northwestern University Press, 1939-1949).

9. Brown et al. "The child's grammar from I to III."

10. Lois Bloom, *Language development: Form and function in emerging grammars* (Cambridge, Mass.: M.I.T. Press, 1970).

11. Brendan O. Webster, and David Ingram, "The comprehension and production of the anaphoric pronouns he, she, him, her in normal and linguistically deviant children," *Papers and reports on child language development* (Stanford, Calif.: Stanford University, 1972), pp. 55-77.

12. John B. Carroll, "Development of native language skills beyond the early years," in *The learning of language,* edited by Carroll E. Reed (New York: Appleton-Century-Crofts, 1971), p. 130.

13. H.G. Birch and L. Belmont, "Auditory-visual integration, intelligence, and reading ability in school children," *Perceptual and Motor Skills* 20 (1965): 295-305.

14. Jacqueline J. Goodnow, "Matching auditory and visual series: modality problem or translation problem?" *Child Development* 42 (1971):1187-1201.

15. Jacqueline J. Goodnow, "The role of modalities in perceptual and cognitive development," in *Minnesota Symposia on Child Psychology,* vol. 5, edited by John P. Hill (Minneapolis: The University of Minnesota Press, 1971), pp. 3-28.

16. D.C. Kendall, "Language and communication problems in children," in *Speech pathology,* edited by R.W. Rieber and R.S. Brubaker (Amsterdam: North-Holland Publishing Co., 1966), pp. 285-98.

17. Slobin, "Cognitive prerequisites for the development of grammar."

18. D.O. Hebb, W.E. Lambert, and G.R. Tucker, "Language, thought and experience," *Modern Language Journal,* 54 (1971):212-22.

19. D.O. Hebb, W.E. Lambert, and G.R. Tucker, "A DMZ in the language war," *Psychology Today* 6 (1973):55-62.
20. Ibid., p. 62.
21. Slobin, "Cognitive prerequisites for the development of grammar."
22. Susan M. Ervin-Tripp, "Some strategies for the first two years," in *Language acquisition and communicative choice: Essays by Susan Ervin-Tripp*, edited by Anwar S. Dil (Stanford, California: Stanford University Press, 1973), pp. 204-238.
23. Courtney B. Cazden, *Child language and education.* (New York: Holt, Rinehart and Winston, Inc., 1972).
24. John B. Carroll, "Factors in verbal achievement," in *Proceedings of the 1961 Invitational Conference on Testing Problems,* edited by P.L. Dressel (Princeton: Educational Testing Service, 1962), pp. 11-18.
25. Vera John, "Cognitive development in the bilingual child," in *Report of the 21st Annual Round Table Meeting on Linguistics and Language Studies,* edited by James E. Alatis (Washington, D.C.: Georgetown University Press, 1970), pp. 59-67.
26. John B. Carroll "Language and psychology," in *Linguistics Today,* edited by Archibald A. Hill (New York: Basic Books, 1969), p. 165.
27. C.R. Seligman, G.R. Tucker, and W.E. Lambert, "The effects of speech style and other attributes on teachers' attitudes toward pupils," *Language in Society,* 1972, 1:131-42.
28. Richard Hendrickson, "Pygmalion revisited," Paper read at Linguistics Symposium, California State Polytechnic University, March 31, 1973.
29. Slobin, "Cognitive prerequisites for the development of grammar," p. 193.

2 Leslie's Development

Leslie is a half American Indian, half Caucasian girl, past five years of age at this writing. Her adoptive parents have had her since she was two months old. She is an unusually attractive little girl, looks very alert and bright, and has a happy disposition. She is large for her age, but nicely proportioned.

Leslie's Family

Leslie's parents are white, middle-class, and college-educated. Her father is director of advertising for a large industrial firm. Her mother is a musician and pianist by training and education, but spends full time as a homemaker. Some of her volunteer activities have had an effect on Leslie by affording her additional experiences. While Leslie was four her mother worked in the children's department at their church, taking Leslie along for an early session on Sunday mornings, at which time Leslie participated in activities with school age children for an hour before going to her own class. While Leslie was 3;7 to 5;4 her mother worked as a classroom volunteer in their neighborhood school. Most of the work was done while Leslie was in nursery school, but because of classroom schedules, Leslie attended the third-grade classroom with her mother for two hours a week for several months, at the teacher's suggestion.

Leslie's family is child-oriented. Vacations and weekly activities are planned to give the children desirable experiences. The children are provided with an abundance of good toys and books. More than an average amount of time is spent with the children, talking to them, reading to them, playing games with them, and helping them with a variety of projects such as cooking and art projects. The home environment approaches the ideal in most ways.

The only other child in her family is Fred, who was born into the family, is three years, four months older than Leslie is. The personalities and speech development of the two children have been very different. Fred was a thin, active baby who cooed, babbled, and made noises of all kinds. From about six months on, whenever a family member would look at Fred and talk to him, he would respond by babbling, giving the impression that he thought he was talking. By about eight months, he had developed English intonation patterns to go with his babbling. He was a prolific talker from the beginning, and as soon as he had a few words, they were articulated clearly enough that strangers could usually understand what he was trying to say. By the time he was 2 years, 5 months (2;5) he was engaging in conversation such as, "Shall we go to the

9

restaurant? Shall we talk to the Jack-in-the-Box? I want a hamboogoo, two tacos, some French fries and a coke." (He was pretending he was giving his order to the Jack-in-the-Box.) Hamburger was one of the few words he did not articulate clearly.

Fred used language in original ways at an early age. For example, at 2;6 Fred saw a flock of birds at the train station. The birds had been on the roof of a building and suddenly they flew toward a parked freight car and each of the birds momentarily lit on the roof of the car, then flew off again in a flock. He said, "Oh, look at the birds dancing on the train." Or looking at San Francisco Bay, he asked "Why is the water wrinkled?" (with waves). At 4;1, when someone said to Fred, "I guess I'm getting old," he said impishly, "You look pretty new to me." It was the first pun noted by the investigator, but from then on, many were noted. Fred's language development follows the usual stereotype of the bright child (at the end of the second grade Fred's I.Q. was 138 as measured at school).

Fred was thin and wiry, average in height, and slightly less than average in weight for his age. While he always had excellent small muscle coordination, his large muscle coordination was not unusually good and he was never very fond of vigorous activities, such as skating and bike riding.

At pre-school age particularly, Fred was not as well adjusted socially as Leslie. While both children were capable of entertaining themselves for long periods of time, Leslie sought out playmates whenever possible and enjoyed them whereas Fred, given a choice, played alone, usually working on projects of many kinds.

Leslie's Non-Linguistic Development

Leslie was a large baby and has continued to be tall for her age, falling within the 99th percentile of girls her age, as measured at her annual medical examination. While she was still four years old and visiting in the first-grade class, she was among the larger children in the room. She has good muscle coordination, both large and small, and could perform all the classroom tasks with the first-graders, as well as doing the same things they did on the playground. She learned to roller skate and ride a bike very easily whereas Fred has some difficulty. At 2;11 Leslie could thread heavy cord (such as carpet thread) through the small hole of a wheel from a car. In general, she worked easily with her hands.

Leslie was considered to be rather late in walking. She was 14 months before she walked alone. Previous to that, she walked well if someone held her hands, but she did not seem to have the confidence to do it alone.

Fred, on the other hand, walked by himself at 11½ months, and had been taking steps alone for a month or six weeks previous to that. He seemed willing to experiment and fall down and get up again, but Leslie was not.

She always liked her room to be neat. If she found toys strewn around on the floor of her room before she went to bed at night, she would say "Meth!" 'mess' (3;0) and immediately start throwing toys into her toy box.

At this same age she would typically concentrate on one activity for long periods of time. She would frequently sit at her little table in front of a floor length window in the family room for an hour or an hour and a half and make things with play dough or other such activities.

Leslie always had a keen sense of humor, both from the point of view of seeing what was amusing in events around her and a capability of making others laugh. She was considered to be the family clown at an early age because of her tendency to make amusing noises and perform in ways designed to entertain the family.

From about three years of age on, Leslie was able to carry a tune well and enjoyed music. She enjoyed rhythm instruments, listening to music, and has progressed quite well with piano lessons. At 4;8 she asked her mother if she could learn to play the piano, so her mother started giving her lessons on request—there was no schedule.

In many ways Leslie's development seemed to be average or above. For example, at 2;9 she was drawing people that included eyes, nose, mouth, a body, plus four straight lines for the arms and legs, which she identified as hands and feet. At 2;11 she started adding hair. At this same age and for several more months, Fred's people lacked arms and legs. In nursery school, Fred's mother considered his pictures to be inferior to those of most of the other children in his class. However, from the first grade on, his teachers have considered him to be an exceptionally good artist as compared to the other children in his classes.

Both of the children learned to count and to recognize the letters of the alphabet before they were three. Leslie watched "Sesame Street" on TV and received much of her instruction in letters and numbers there.

At about 3;0 she started to recognize letter shapes in nature or in drawings, or she would shape a piece of string into a K-like figure, for example, and then name it "K." Tree branches were a favorite place for her to discover letter-shapes.[a] Once she had thoroughly learned the alphabet, her interest in letters per se subsided.

---

[a]Christian,[1] reporting on the language development of Raquel, a Spanish-English bilingual child who had learned to recognize the letters of the alphabet and to spell a few words, says,

> During this period from twenty to twenty-five months she seemed to live in a world of letters, discovering them on signs, in newspapers, and through her environment—although largely in English sets, of course. For example, at twenty-two months she was so impressed by the huge letters spelling out SAFEWAY on a store that she cried to climb up and play with them. . . . From the age of twenty-five to twenty-eight months, although play with words and letters continued on much the same basis as before, generally with Raquel's father, her interest in both letters and words declined steadily.

It could also be said of Leslie that "she seemed to live in a world of letters" for several months. Letters and their shapes appear to hold a fascination for the two-year-old that they do not hold for the five- or six-year old. For this reason, it appears to be a desirable age to introduce the alphabet.

By 2;10 she appeared to have the concept of number. When offered a cookie, she asked /tr/? 'May I have two?' and then she took two. And when shown a picture with a pond and sailboats on it, she was asked "How many boats are there?" She counted

/wun tr thE thOr thI/   'One, two, three, four, five.'   (2;10)

There were indeed five boats. When counting, she pointed to one object as she said one number (we have watched some children point randomly as they count, not seeming to connect numbers, which they have memorized in the proper order, with the items being pointed to). At 5;0 skill with numbers was about first-grade level: she added and subtracted with numbers up to 10 easily.

Leslie has displayed a remarkable memory for events that took place at very early points in her life. For example, at 4;1 she reported,

When I was a baby, I was in my crib and I was on my wall, I just
     pickeded up my toys and chewed on them.   (4;1)

The investigator asked for a clarification about the crib being on the wall. Leslie asserted it was *her* wall (not just *any* wall), and as to how it got there, she said,

Well, must be tied or hammered on there. I think it was
     hammered on.   (4;1)

When she was 14 months old her crib was dismantled and was given away. From her position in the crib, she was not aware of the legs of the crib. An impression such as this is something obviously not passed along to her by family members, as early memories are often thought to be.

When Leslie was 2;1 Leslie's family decided, for a variety of reasons, that they would give away their dog, and the investigator offered to do the physical transporting of the dog to its new home. Leslie observed this, but said nothing at all. At 2;1 she was very limited as to what she could say about it. At 3;3, she angrily accused the investigator of having taken the dog away without permission (see p. 112, Chapter 7).

These are only two examples from many that could be cited of her long-term memory for events that transpired during very early speech periods, but which were not discussed by Leslie until much later, and which had not been discussed at all in Leslie's presence in the interim.

Pre-school and School Experience

Fred and Leslie both started to read about the time they were four years old. Leslie had learned to read many words before she was four, and at 3;11

she read her first story. It was one her mother wrote using words that Leslie was familiar with. They were based on sound patterns used on "Sesame Street," a TV program that both Fred and Leslie watched regularly. By the time she was 5;0 she could read simple stories easily and could 'sound out' new words of two and three syllables.

The reading process seemed to offer a constant stream of surprises for Leslie. When someone was sitting beside her as she read, she often asked for help with words she didn't recognize. Or when someone else was reading to her, she followed the print as the reading proceeded, and she would often go back a few words and ask, pointing, "What's that word?" Sometimes she registered surprise by saying "Oh!," but the look on her face was the most accurate clue to the revelation that the written word was to her. She asked about both functors and content words.

She came to be convinced that knowing how to spell a word was the sure way of knowing how to pronounce it. Her usual pronunciation of *Ernie*, one of the muppets on Sesame Street, was *Ornie*. She had an Ernie muppet (puppet) of her own, and the investigator asked her what his name was. She said "Ornie," and the investigator repeated it after he. 'No!" she said, "Not Ornie. *E R N I E!*" (3;11). She spelled out the name (in a very loud voice), assuming that if a person knew how to spell it, they would know how to pronounce it.

On another occasion, she said /biksit/ for *biscuit*. The investigator said, "Can you say /bis+kit/?" pronouncing it slowly with a boundary between the two syllables. "No, I can't," she said, " 'cause I don't know how to spell it!" The word was spelled for her, and she asked, "Like a doctor kit?" "That's right." She said it three times, and the third time it was correct. It doesn't seem likely that the spelling of the second syllable, in particular, could be of much help to a four-year-old in pronouncing *biscuit*. This is offered as an example of her faith that spelling is illuminating in the process of pronunciation.

It is interesting to note that the spelling of irregular past tense verbs in stories she read did not noticeably affect her continued regularization of them. For example, one day in her reading she came to *knew* and asked what it was. The answer left her just as puzzled as she had been before she asked. The investigator hesitatingly said, "You usually say *knowed*." Leslie said "Oh!" and read it *knowed*.

On some occasions the printed word even bolstered her faith in her morphological rules, e.g., when she started reading *said,* no one could convince her that it was not properly pronounced *sayed*. This was her past tense form for *say*, and *said* certainly didn't look like /sed/ to her. When she read aloud (much of her reading was silent) she varied between reading the inflected verb form as printed and translating it to follow her own rules. It did not, however, appear to make a difference in her own spontaneous productions of these regularized forms.

An example of her reading at 4;7 follows:

> The Rabbit and the Turtle. A rabbit keeped saying, "I am the
> fastest runner of all. A turtle got tired of hearing him. He
> sayed . . . How come you won't read to me? (4;7)

The functors were all there, articulated clearly, but the past tense verbs were her own. *Kept* is similar to *said* in that it has a final dental serving as a past-tense marker. The vowel change is not the principal marker of tense as in *sing/sang*, for example.

At this same age, the functors, as a rule, in Leslie's spontaneous speech were much less well specified:

> And here a grill, and there's a mountains right there. (4;7)

> Just made a house out a dem.   (4;7)

Of and *the* were typical of the functors that an unstressed vowel was substituted for at this age. However, there were no functors that she did not clearly enunciate and use appropriately upon occasion by this age. It may be that the omission of the copula in the first clause of the compound sentence above is an example of her continued uncertainty about its role. Where *grill* is singular, the copula is omitted, but where *mountain* is plural, it is inserted. This *s* may be serving as a plural marker for her rather than as a copula.

It may have been just coincidence that this improvement in her pronunciation of many words and her rapid improvement in the use of functors occurred soon after she started to read. The author is convinced, however, that the reading process helped the speech process, at least in the area of phonology.

The first few months of Leslie's first year in nursery school (3;7 to 4;4) were not entirely successful. Her first teacher was one who viewed nursery school as preparation for a highly structured classroom which she assumed the children would be promoted into, even though this was only the first year of a two-year nursery school program. Everyone was required to sit still and do certain things in certain ways at certain times and not speak out of turn. Art projects were pre-drawn and pre-planned for the child to complete. While some children seemed to function well under the stern supervision and constant direction of this teacher, Leslie rebelled, and resorted more and more frequently as time went on to pretending to be a baby or an animal, going around on her hands and knees, making appropriate noises. Her objective was to be some creature who was unable to participate in classroom activities. Her mother took her out of this class and found a more relaxed atmosphere for her where she did very well.

During Leslie's second year in nursery school (4;7 to 5;4) her teacher often asked her to read a story to the class, either something from a book or the story printed at the bottom of slide-projected pictures. Leslie did this easily, accepting the assignment from the teacher without objection. She objected regularly, however, to reading for the investigator. Reading had never been presented as a test or a task that she needed to perform for any reason, and she clearly preferred to be read to.

The third-grade classroom, mentioned above, that Leslie visited with her mother was an open classroom. Learning centers were set up at different tables in the room and at certain times during the day the children were allowed to choose from among these activities. At the times when the teacher told the children to choose a center, Leslie made her choice, along with the third-graders, and performed as well as they did. Sometimes she chose a center where children were learning to measure quantities (the end result being Kool-Aid, which the children could then drink, or something else edible), reading books for fun, working puzzles, or writing a puppet play. Leslie was able to read and follow instructions where this was necessary. She worked nicely with the other children, and they appeared to accept her as another third-grader, perhaps not noticing her spasmodic attendance.

The kindergarten teacher, and the teacher whose class Leslie had visited, were convinced that Leslie should not spend a year in kindergarten but that she should go directly from nursery school to first grade. They persuaded the principal of the school and surprised Leslie's family with the announcement that it was arranged for her to be in the first grade.

There is no obvious way that Leslie's early slowness in speech development has adversely affected her performance in early school activities.

Early Language Development

Leslie's speech development was noticeably slow, particularly compared to her other capabilities, during her earliest years. Between the ages of four and five, Leslie's speech development caught up in most ways, as will be discussed below. It was only at the earliest stages of speech development that her speech development was noticeably slower than that of other average-to-bright children.

During her pre-speech development, she didn't babble very much. If a family member talked to her at 0;5 to 0.9, she would be almost certain to laugh in response, but seldom responded with babbling. When she did, toward the end of this period, she used intonation contours similar to Fred's, but her 'sentences' were usually shorter.

Her earliest speech period was characterized by frustration because her family couldn't understand her. After a first try, she often took a person by the hand and showed them what she was talking about, if this was feasible. In many instances, there was no way she could make her meaning clear, and she cried or shouted. At 1;9 and also much earlier, her typical reactions to being unable to make herself understood were to jabber in a loud voice, with such sounds as 'bawbawbaw' but with no recognizable words. These sounds were clipped, and were almost always accompanied by rather jerky movements of her body and arms, such as stretching her arm out and pointing her finger, or clenching her fist. She did this on such occasions as when someone tried to feed her and she wanted to feed herself, or when the dog tried to take something away from her, or someone tried to give her something she didn't want, not having understood her request. By *clipped*, we mean sounds which are produced with greater tenseness and stronger expiration and at a more rapid tempo than unmarked speech sounds. Consonants tended to be unvoiced, e.g., /b/ approached the voicelessness of a /p/, and vowels tended to be shorter in duration than in unmarked speech. The use of this marking of speech by Leslie could be considered to be a register that signifies impatience. With Leslie, clipped sounds were almost invariably accompanied by additional loudness of speech also.

Between 0;7 and 0;8 and continuing through 3;0 she imitated a number of non-language sounds, such as an airplane overhead, a dog barking, a bird singing, a siren, a fly buzzing, a car starting, or numerous other sounds. She would imitate the sound immediately upon hearing it, look steadily at the person with whom she was 'conversing' as though to say "I hear a siren," or whatever she was imitating, and wait for a response such as, "Oh, yes, there's a siren, isn't there?" Only after her remark had been answered would she go on with her own activities. It clearly called for a reply. Gradually, as she acquired the lexicon, she began substituting the word instead of the imitation: if she heard an airplane, she stopped what she was doing, went to the window and said /pwAn/ 'airplane!' and then waited for someone to reply, "Oh, yes, there's an airplane, isn't there?" Her hearing seemed to be unusually keen, for she was often the first in the family to hear these sounds.

Halliday's definition of an "utterance,"[2] based on function, specifies that in order for a vocalization by the child to be considered as an utterance (i.e., as language) there must be "an observable and constant relation between content and expression, such that, for each content/expression pair, the expression was observed in at least three unambiguous instances and the content was interpretable in functional terms." Using this criterion, the imitations may be classified as language, just as the lexical items following them are, for they function in just the same way. In Halliday's system of developmental function of Phase I (the child's initial functional-linguistic system), this would fall in the category of serving an interactional function, 'me and you,' expressing a desire to share common information.

Other than the language just described, Leslie began using words, or monoremes, at 11 months. In this study, the term monoreme will be used rather than *word* for Leslie's first utterances. Bean[3] mentions that A.F. Chamberlain[4] was the first to use this term to refer to functionally sentential utterances which consist of one vocally articulated unit. Gregoire[5] and Werner and Kaplan, among others, also use the term. The latter define it:

> Among the global expressions of the child, which consist of bodily movements and vocalizations, there emerge certain ones which, in some way, *refer* to a situation rather than being solely interjectional, that is, expressive of addressor-attitudes towards it. Such patterns, insofar as they include a discriminable, vocally articulated element ("vocable"), have usually been designated 'one-word sentences.' This term, however, does not seem appropriate in view of the fact that these utterances are actually neither words nor sentences: they are indeed prior to the correlative emergence of both word and sentence forms. For this reason, we shall designate these early one-unit referential patterns as *monoremes*.[6]

They add:

> Though, to be sure, monoremes characteristically refer to total happenings and never to precisely delimited components such as action per se or thing per se, the beginnings of such an implicit 'categorization' of events through vocal expression seem to form, closely tied up with the attitude governing the expression. Thing-dominant monoremes appear, occurring most often in a quasi-declarative attitude [Halliday's instrumental function], while activity-dominant monoremes began to occur, most often in a request-demand attitude [Halliday's regulatory function].[7]

Throughout this study the term *monoreme* will be used with essentially the meaning given above.

Using this definition, Leslie had five monoremes at 0;11, all reduplications, which were:

/dada/	'daddy'
/momo/	'mommy'
/gogo/	'doggie'
/baba/	'pattycake'
/gaga/	an expression of happiness.

(See Ferguson, Peizer and Weeks for a fuller discussion of these five monoremes.[8])

Ervin-Tripp and Miller say "The child's first word normally appears before the first birthday, but a year may pass before the child forms his first two-word sentence."[9] With five words at 0;11, then, Leslie was not slow in starting the speech process. Hinckley, for example, reports a case of a girl who was 5;6 and entering kindergarten but "seemed unable to utter a word, though she was not deaf."[10] This appears to be a pathological case, and is not similar in any way to Leslie's slow speech development problem.

A case of slow speech development is reported by Nice in which her daughter R's first word, 'er-er,' denoting a pig, came at 1;4.[11] R's vocabulary at 2;0 consisted of five words, the same number Leslie had at 0;11.

Nice studied some other cases of slow speech development and enumerates ways in which she thinks the speech of slow developers differs from that of normal speech development:

1. Absence of inflection
2. Omission of minor words (functors)
3. Small size of vocabulary
4. Infantile stammer
5. The presence of original expression.

From the cases she studied, the failure to inflect words and the omission of copulas and articles were present in 9 out of 12 cases. These were children with normal intelligence but slow speech development. While Leslie was not late in getting a start, as R was, she did exhibit at least three of these five distinguishing features of slow speech developers of Nice's: absence of inflection, omission of minor words, and presence of original expression. While it was difficult to measure Leslie's productive vocabulary size, and number of content words she produced appeared to be normal in range, in spite of her dependence on multi-purpose words (see Chapter 5). The multi-purpose words often substituted for lexical items Leslie produced on previous occasions, but appeared not to be able to recall at the desired moment. Her passive vocabulary was unquestionably large. At 3;0, R had "a vocabulary of less than 50 words, one thirtieth the size of the average of published vocabularies for this age."[12] It is possible, however, that this was not a fair evaluation of R's vocabulary at that time, since Nice mentions that before R was three years old "she had what practically amounted to a language of her own that was understood by almost nobody." This is reminiscent of Leslie, and is one of the reasons that no attempts were made to count vocabulary. Leslie had many lexical items, if one considers her intended meanings. It is another matter that they did not match the adult system phonologically and were therefore often not understood. There is a qualitative difference between children who simply do not have lexical items, and those who have them but can't produce them understandably.

As for the infantile stammer mentioned by Nice, some of the /E/'s and

/A/'s discussed in Chapter 5 may be accounted for in this way. This is not an involuntary stuttering, but a use of speech sounds while appearing to search for a word or phrase.

By "original expression" (item 5 above), Nice is presumably referring to language such as Leslie's "That /winding/?" meaning 'What's that blowing in the wind?' (3;5), or "When I heard the bell ring, I quicked out," meaning "I ran out quickly,' (5;7), where she changes the form class, first a noun to a verb, and second, an adverb to a verb. (Chapter 6 discusses Leslie's inclination not to distinguish form classes.) Later examples of non-adult expression include: "What do you think I am—of grader?" meaning 'What grade do you think I'm in?' (5;7) (she wasn't sure the investigator knew she was in the first grade), and "Do you want to see something of me funny?" (in analogy perhaps with 'Do you want to see some of my books?') meaning 'Do you want to see me do something funny?' (5;9). *Original expression* appears to be an appropriate term for much of Leslie's speech. Not having learned to pattern her speech after the adult system to the extent that many children, such as Fred, do, she must search for original ways of expressing her meanings. Where language is concerned, this may appear to be undesirable; it seems that there are only a limited number of acceptable ways to be 'creative' with language.

Sastri discusses degrees of creativity and labels as deviances such uses of language as a change in form class, such as the use of a noun as a verb, and metaphors and personifications are labeled 'violation of selectional rules.'[13] These are also listed among the most creative of linguistic activities because they are the least repetitive. The author argues that the most grammatical sentences are the least creative (according to standard grammar) and the most creative sentences tend to be less formally grammatical. The ways in which Fred was cited as being 'original' in the use of language, i.e., the use of metaphors that appear to be intentional, the change of form class in poetry, and puns, are acceptable forms of creativity in language, however, whereas originality that appears to be unintentional is generally unacceptable. In other activities where there is more latitude than there is in language, this same approach is labeled as 'creative' and is thought of as desirable. It should be noted here that Leslie's teachers and other adults who have watched her work consider her to be a very 'creative child.'

A great deal of research needs to be done, but the question of whether or not the slow speech developers are typically original, or creative, persons, not following the usual patterns in activities other than language, is worth pursuing.

As was mentioned above, Leslie was very difficult to understand, with the exception of a few words such as 'mama' and 'dada,' which were clearly articulated. At 3;0 it was estimated that family members could understand between 25 percent and 50 percent of what she said, partly due to their having learned many of her words. At this age, strangers and even family friends who saw her on an average of two hours a week, didn't understand more than an occasional word or short sentence. Since she first started talking she has talked quite a lot, not as much as Fred, but no one would consider her to be a non-verbal child. She always gave the impression of knowing precisely what she was saying, even though none of it was intelligible to anyone else.

While Fred enjoyed using long words and adult-type phrases, Leslie made no apparent effort in this direction.

The features of Leslie's speech that contributed most to making her difficult to understand were: (1) her use of vowels without consonants—many utterances seemed to consist of just strings of vowels; (2) her lack of final consonants in words where an initial consonant was present; (3) her use of consonant harmony rule—in words of two syllables, the initial consonant of both syllables was the same; and (4) the wide variation in the production of vowel sounds, even in words that were easily understandable, such as 'mama' (see Chapter 4).

Beginning at about 2;10 she seemed to be making a conscious effort to add final consonants, adding *quick* to her active lexicon, and soon thereafter adding the /k/ to *milk*, which had been /br/. It became /mrk/ at this point. Velars were among the first stop consonants she acquired in initial position, and also in final position.

Partly because of this slow acquisition of consonant sounds, her parents had been concerned about her hearing (despite her keen hearing of non-speech sounds) and her comprehension. Her pediatrician tested her hearing and pronounced it excellent, and family members devised various ways to test her comprehension. They would ask her to go to the kitchen, for example, and bring back a certain item. She invariably followed instructions.

Many times when family members would try to get her to say a word more clearly, and would articulate it slowly and carefully for her, she would watch their mouth and then make an obvious effort to imitate the lip and tongue movements, almost invariably with poor results—her word would sound less like the model instead of more like it.

Morphological Development

Leslie followed the usual pattern (Ervin-Tripp[14]) of first using the irregular plural and past tense forms, such as *feet* and *went*, and later, when she formed a rule governing the regularization of plural and past-tense forms, she dropped the correct irregular forms and used her rule to regularize all noun plurals and past-tense verbs, e.g., *foots* and *goed*. While Ervin-Tripp and Miller point out that "a six-year-old often uses forms such as *buyed* and *bought*, or *brang* and *brought* interchangeably,"[15] at 4;7 Leslie was using such forms much more frequently than other children her age when measured for grammatical immaturities on a story retelling task (see Chapter 3). By the time she is six it is expected that she will be using the adult forms as consistently as the average child.

It is interesting to speculate, however, on the difference in her attitude about her willingness, even eagerness, to bring her pronunciation more closely in line with the adult system. As mentioned above in connection with her reading, and also with self-drilling (see Chapter 4), and with frequent self-corrections in conversation, she demonstrated her awareness of her failure to match the adult models. Her phonological rules may be thought of as unintentional rules—a scheme by which she made the most of her capabilities at any given time, e.g., a two-syllable word: CV + Voiceless Velar VC → Voiced Velar V + Voiceless Velar V (C),[b] e.g., Mickey → giki. But even while she used the rule, she was open to suggestions and help in changing it. Her morphological rules seem more like intentional rules. She was so sure she was right that seeing the irregular form in a book, e.g., *knew*, or having someone tell her *knowed* was wrong, or hearing others use the adult form, could not shake her confidence in her own system, e.g., past tense → *d* (or *ed* as in have-ed, her past tense for *have*). The phonological rules were substitution rules, and she was aware she was substituting something of her own into the adult system. The morphological rules did not appear to function to substitute something of her own into the adult system; she saw these rules as being the correct system, and if adults didn't agree with her, it was because they were wrong. It is not apparent how aware other children are of their phonological immaturities, but other children seem to resist changes in their morphological rules just as strongly as Leslie did.

At 4;7 Leslie was beginning to use *had*; her self-corrections indicated her uncertainty about the form:

> I had . . . uh, I haved . . . a had a motorcycle and I sit down and
>   thinking what I was doing and lookin' at all those kids and
>   teacher goed by and didn't ask me anything.   (4;7)

Later in the same conversation:

> I haved all of 'em.   (4;7)

> I wish I haved a football hat and a football.   (4;7)

At this same age, Leslie told a story which included the following regularized verbs:

> He was a good little dog and once he *heared* a big "Ruff, ruff."
>   . . . So the baby got up and *eated* his breakfast . . . Klunk
>   *goed* the chair . . . He *knowed* that somebody lived there

---

[b]In linguistic notation, a symbol enclosed in parentheses indicates that this feature is optional, e.g., (C) in the example above indicates that the word may, or may not, end in a final consonant.

already . . . They *maked* up a tent and they lived in that
tent . . . He *falled* on the floor. (4;7)

This story consisted of 501 words. A count of the six regularized verbs
above indicates she used *goed* 5 times, *eated* 3 times, *heared* 2 times, and *maked*,
knowed, and *falled* once each. However, at this point she was also beginning
to make correct use again of some irregular verbs, as well as some incorrect
irregular verbs:

The owl didn't know anyhow that owl *swang* in some honey
they had. (4;7)

The baby dog . . . there was a strong wind and it *flew* the baby
dog away almost cause they were under a tent. (4;7)

It *broke*. (4;7)

Earlier Leslie had used the form *swinged* for the past tense of *swing*, so this
indicates a change in her rules. It is quite certain that she had not heard the
form *swang* from family members. Whether she heard it from friends or not, it
represents a rule change for her.

In the example above in which Leslie used *flew*, she meant *blew*, the
semantic difference being in the instrument of the action. It is apparent that
she did not assume the dog knew how to fly, but that the wind was the instrument causing the action. Therefore, it is an incorrect lexical choice, but interesting in that the present tense forms, *blow* and *fly* are not phonetically similar,
and that she had previously used both *blowed* and *flied* without confusion for
the past tense forms, indicating a lexical storage problem.

In this story of Leslie's, *broke* was the only irregular past-tense form she
used correctly, and again, she had used *breaked* at earlier ages.

In this story, *maked* was used only once, but this was her usual past tense
for *make*. However, *made* was used regularly with the progressive *-ing*, both
earlier and later than the following examples at 4;2:

Know what I mading now? I mading a fish now.

She also used it for the infinitive:

I going to made a person. I going to made a ear.

The progression of Leslie's morphological development, on the whole, followed patterns reported for other children. In the middle of her fifth year this
appeared to be the principal aspect of language acquisition in which she could

still be said to be 'slow.' This is based on the comparison of her performance on the story retelling task, as discussed above.

Development of Speech Registers and Paralinguistic Features

Frequent observations were made during the course of the data collection for this research on Leslie's speech registers and paralinguistic development. At earliest stages, this has been reported elsewhere,[16,17] and will be reviewed briefly here.

The term *speech register* is used here as defined by Halliday, McIntosh, and Strevens.[18] They state that speech varieties in a language community consist of varieties according to user—that is, varieties in the sense that each speaker uses one variety and uses it all the time—and varieties according to use—that is, in the sense that each speaker has a range of varieties and chooses between them at different times. The variety according to user is a *dialect*, and the variety according to use is a *register*. Speech registers function to convey information or emotion beyond that which is conveyed by the words alone.

According to Halliday et al.'s definition, all utterances must be in *some* dialect and in *some* register. What is referred to here as the unmarked register is Leslie's usual conversational register. Most utterances recorded during the course of this study would belong in this category. All other registers can be said to be marked in some way.

Whisper

As was discussed in Weeks,[19] whisper was one of the registers in which Fred, John (their cousin), and Leslie differed the most. Leslie used whispering regularly since she first began to talk. Fred was not observed to use whispering until he was 4;6, at which time he used it for telling secrets. In situations in which speech was forbidden, as when a parent was talking on the telephone or someone was taking a nap in the room, Leslie and John resorted to whispering, whereas Fred used normal voice until about 5;2, at which time he refrained entirely from speaking.

At 1;7 Leslie came into the room where her mother was talking on the telephone. "Bye," she whispered and waved as she left the room. She also carefully observed the rule that one was not to speak in a normal voice when someone was taking a nap. She frequently said "Shhh! Baby sleeping," to family members after putting a doll to bed. If a visitor didn't observe this rule, he was requested to leave the room. On one occasion when Leslie was visiting the investigator's home, and Leslie was supposed to be taking a nap, the investigator lay down, closed her eyes, and pretended to sleep. Leslie said several things in a whisper and got no reply. Then she brought her clothes and placed them beside the investigator, wanting them put on, thus ending her nap. Upon getting no response, she started scolding, whispering just as loud as she could possibly whisper, "Koth on! Koth on!" 'Clothes on!.' She finally resorted to shaking the investigator, trying to awaken her, but still whispering!

Leslie also used whispering for secrets, starting at about 3;0.

Soft voice

Leslie used soft, or low, voice regularly for saying things she was not sure how to pronounce, or was uncertain about in some other respect. This is discussed in Chapter 4 in regard to Leslie's practicing certain words. As her confidence in her pronunciation improved, her volume rose. When she was certain about what she was saying and of her way of saying it, she did not speak softly. Her unmarked volume tended to be comparatively loud. Leslie often stopped to correct herself as she was speaking. Corrections resulted from uncertainty, and these almost always carried soft voice.

Clarification

This is another of the speech registers discussed in Weeks.[20] Fred's and John's clarification included speech that was delivered more slowly and with more careful enunciation than was normal for them. For them it also included the use of full forms as opposed to contractions. At 2;10 Leslie clarified her speech principally by lengthening the vowels, especially the last vowel of the word, and opening her mouth wider than usual. This was apparently in imitation of family members who used this technique for enunciating words more clearly for her. This clarification was a spontaneous one, it was not in response to a request for her to repeat something, or asking what she had said. In this event, she either repeated it exactly as she had said it the first time, or she placed the stress on a different syllable or word. Sometimes clarification consisted of demonstrating what she meant by touching an object, taking the listener by the hand to another room and pointing to what she was talking about. Sometimes the clarification would take the form of an imitative sound. For example, she was telling about what a rabbit in a picture book was doing. She said,

/E dE saw/   'He saws.'   (2;10)

When the investigator made no response, she assumed she had not been understood, and she added,

/E saw E dadE E saw E tztztztztz/   (2;10)

She made the sawing sound with her tongue and teeth, and also moved her arms in imitation of sawing as she made the noise.

Baby talk

Fred and John were observed using high pitch, exaggerated intonation, phonetic modification (consisting principally of pursing the lips, resulting in rounding and fronting of the vowels), and grammatical modification in their baby talk to pets, younger children, and to adults as a means of getting sympathy, or for some similar purpose. Leslie used baby talk frequently when playing with her dolls, not so much in speaking to the dolls or stuffed toys as when pretending the dolls or toys were talking. For example, at 3;4, Leslie had a small doll in the bathtub with her, and she was speaking for the doll:

> Hey!   I can't /   baf/ . . . you can't /ə baf ə mE ku/
>   you too big!   'Hey!   You can't have a bath with me
> because you're too big.'   (3;4)

She corrected herself, having started out talking for herself instead of for the doll. It was all high pitch, and the words were clipped. Rather than pursing her lips for extra rounding, she tightened her lips and the vowels were unrounded and more tense. The consonants were given more aspiration than usual, and the entire passage was more nasal than usual. This was her usual way at this age for her to produce baby talk. However, by 4;1 she had begun to purse her lips and give the vowels extra rounding for baby talk. An example at this age includes Leslie's use of baby talk for reporting something that happened to her when she was younger. Fred and John both used baby talk under these circumstances, too. In this example, Leslie had been telling about how she could 'get out of the fence,' meaning climb over the little fence which was in the doorway to her room. The investigator asked "You could get out of what?"

> Out of a fence. If I was two again.   (4;1)

Thinking about herself being two years old again, she used exaggerated intonation and fronting and rounding of the vowels.

Mimicry

In this study, as well as in previous studies, we have made a distinction between *mimicry* and *imitation*. In child language studies imitation is usually used to refer to a child's repetition of an adult's sentence immediately after the adult says it, either on request or spontaneously. *Mimicry,* as used here, refers to a child's use of a word or phrase he has heard, most likely at some previous time, in which he also reproduces the paralinguistic features that characterized the original production. This is a register that John used a great deal and Leslie used infrequently. There are some examples, however. At 2;11 Leslie was using the toy telephone, answering it with

/eO:O/   'Hello.'   (2;11)

The intonation matched her mother's intonation in answering the telephone with the high intonation on the lengthened /O/ and dropping for the second /O/. Leslie had never answered the telephone herself, and in her own speech, used 'hi,' never 'hello.'

At 3;1 Leslie was playing with her teddy bear, calling him Teddy, and the investigator mentioned that she had a younger brother named Ted who was called Teddy when he was small. Leslie answered,

/wEOwE/   'Really?'   (3;1)

It was more of an exclamation than a question, but she gave it question intonation, as most adults do, and in exact mimicry of her father.

Story-telling

As is mentioned several places in this study, Leslie enjoyed making up stories and telling them. She started doing this before her speech was easily understood, so that only occasional words or phrases could be glossed. She often did this while looking at pictures or picture books. At this early age or at later ages when her stories could be understood, her story-telling consistently had certain characteristics. She used exaggerated intonation patterns, that is, a wider pitch range than was used in unmarked speech. The family members who read stories to her were inclined also to use exaggerated intonation. She also used a wide variety of paralinguistic features in assuming the roles of the characters in her stories, or puppet plays, as the case might be. A robber, for example, would have a loud, low-pitched voice. On one occasion Leslie asked the investigator to take the role of a giant and Leslie explained what the story was about. The investigator assumed the role, saying approximately what was expected, but Leslie said,

No!   Giants are gruff!   (3;6)

Pretending to be ignorant, the investigator asked what she meant, so instead of giving instructions, she gave her rendition of a giant's voice. The principal change was in the lowness of the pitch. Babies, of course, always had high-pitched voices.

She also used imitative sounds along with onomatopoeic words which might or might not have been original. In telling the 500-word story mentioned above, she said,

And suddenly she heared a /shwishwi/ that was wind . . . (4;7)

At this age, she didn't actually imitate a dog barking, if that was what she wanted in a story, although she did at earlier ages. She used stereotyped sounds such as 'ruff ruff.' Her stories included many sound effects.

Leslie was selective about when to use her story-telling register. She always used it when composing her own story, but in retelling a story, such as the *Curious George* task (reported in Chapter 3), she used an unmarked conversation register. While some children in this task did use a story-telling register, Leslie apparently interpreted it as a reporting task, repeating what had been told to her and asking questions about those things she did not understand rather than recreating the story.

It was suggested by Weeks that the development of registers may vary more between children than the development of other aspects of language, such as syntax.[21] While Leslie's development of most aspects of speech has been slow, her acquisition of registers and her general mastery of paralinguistic features appears to be advanced for her age, though there is little basis for comparison of Leslie with children other than Fred and John.

Discussion

This chapter has touched on many aspects of Leslie's development, both linguistic and non-linguistic, in an effort to present a fairly complete picture of this bright, happy child who was aware at an early age that her speech development was not keeping pace with her needs nor with that of friends her own size. Leslie made use of a number of strategies to circumvent or overcome the problems she encountered in speech production. Some of these strategies were:

1. To simplify her phonological system by the use of consonant harmony or omission of consonants (see Chapter 4).
2. To drill herself on hard words (see Chapter 4).
3. To rely on paralinguistic features and gestures to offer distinctions made structurally in adult speech (discussed in this chapter and in Chapter 7).
4. To use multi-purpose words to substitute for functors as well as some content words (see Chapters 5 and 8).
5. To rely in some cases on fixed syntactic structures, such as her "Watch-me" imperative construction (see Chapter 6).

It is impossible to say what effect these apparent strategies had on Leslie's speech development, but whereas Leslie's speech development was slow at early ages, by age 5 it could no longer be labeled 'slow,' even though she still did not have the same degree of productive mastery of her language that Fred, for example, had at that age.

Notes

1. Chester C., Christian Jr., "Differential response to language stimuli before age 3: A case study," in *Conference on child language,* Chicago, Nov. 22-24, 1971 (Quebec: Les Presses de l'Universite Laval, 1971), pp. 1-14.
2. M.A.K. Halliday, "Learning how to mean," in *Foundations of language development: A multidisciplinary approach,* edited by Eric and Elizabeth Lenneberg, UNESCO and IBRO, forthcoming.
3. C.H. Bean, "An unusual opportunity to investigate the psychology of language," *Journal of Genetic Psychology,* 1932, 40:181-202.
4. A.F. Chamberlain and I.C. Chamberlain, "Studies of a child. I-IV," *Pedagogical Seminary,* 1904, 11:264-91.
5. A. Gregoire, *L'apprentissage du langage.* 2 vols (Paris: Droz, 1937-1947).
6. Heinz Werner, and Bernard Kaplan, *Symbol formation* (New York: Wiley and Sons, 1963), p. 134.
7. Ibid., p. 137.
8. Charles A. Ferguson, David B. Peizer, and Thelma E. Weeks, "Model-and-replica phonological grammar of a child's first words," *Lingua,* 1973, 31:35-65.
9. Susan M. Ervin-Tripp, and Wick R. Miller, "Language development," in *Child psychology, 62nd yearbook, National Society for the Study of Education,* Part I, edited by H.W. Stevenson, 1963, pp. 108-43.
10. A.C. Hinckley, "A case of retarded speech development," *Pedagogical Seminary,* 1915, 22:121-46.
11. Margaret Nice, "A child who would not talk," *Pedagogical Seminary,* 1925, 32:105-44.
12. Ibid., p. 144.
13. M.I. Sastri, "Degrees of creativity," *Language Sciences,* 1973, No. 27:26-28.
14. Susan M. Ervin-Tripp, "Imitation and structural change in children's language," *New directions in the study of language,* edited by Eric H. Lenneberg, (Cambridge, Mass.: M.I.T. Press, 1964), pp. 163-89.
15. Ervin-Tripp and Miller, "Language development," p. 125.
16. Thelma E. Weeks, "The process of speech socialization in children," unpublished paper, 1969.
17. Thelma E. Weeks, "Speech registers in young children," *Child Development,* 1971, 42:1119-31.

18. M.A.K. Halliday, A. McIntosh, and P.D. Strevens, *The linguistic sciences and language teaching* (London: Longmans, Green, 1964).
19. Weeks, "Speech registers in young children."
20. Ibid.
21. Ibid.

3

Data Collection and Testing

Method of Data Collection

The data have been gathered by means of tape recordings and written notes at irregular time intervals, ranging from twice weekly to bi-monthly from Leslie's fifth month to 5;3. From Leslie's second month until she was 3;11, the investigator visited her home every Thursday, with the exception of vacation periods, for an hour or more. From the second to the fifth months, no tapes were made of Leslie's pre-speech sounds. During the earliest time period, the investigator was studying Fred's speech development, and Leslie's inclusion on the tapes was secondary. However, from about 2;0 on, a concerted effort was made to record Leslie's speech, sometimes in conversation with Fred, and sometimes in other situations. During the period from 2;0 to about 2;9, there were many recording sessions at which either no speech of Leslie's was recorded, or no speech that was glossable was recorded. She often played silently. At these times, urging her to talk was futile. After 3;11 the visits were not scheduled on an every-Thursday basis, but the investigator spent as much or more total time with her as previously (see table 3-1 for a chart of transcriptions and tests).

Bloom reports that she recorded the activities of her three subjects while playing with a group of toys and books, which she took to the homes of the children; while eating; and while playing with a peer.[1] The Berkeley children and the Harvard children had similar routines. Because our interests extended beyond the syntactic development of the children (Leslie, Fred, and their cousins John and Gregory) into speech usage patterns (see Weeks[2]), a special effort was made to vary the setting and the individuals with whom the children talked in order to elicit a full range of their speech capabilities. Recording sessions took place in Leslie's home, the investigator's home and office, parks, airports, restaurants, and other public places. Leslie was also brought into the investigator's home for two- and three-day periods on numerous occasions, during which bath time and bed time activities were recorded. Leslie was recorded in quiet play situations where her speech was essentially private, and other situations in which she was addressing her dolls and stuffed animals, seemingly unaware of the investigator's presence. Verbal interchange took place with all members of her family, her neighborhood friends, with strangers, both adults and children, as well as with the investigator. Leslie was also recorded talking to her dog and her cat. During conversation with the investigator, she was sometimes encouraged to make up stories—at earliest ages, by

31

Table 3-1

Record of Testing and Spontaneous Speech Data Collected on Leslie

Age	Amount of Speech Data	Tests Given and/or Material Elicited (or attempted) Reported in Chapter 3 Unless Specified Otherwise
0;4-0;11	4 hours	
1;0-1;5	2 hours	
1;6-1;8	3 hours	
1;9-1;11	2 hours	
2;0-2;2	4 hours	Began informal phonological testing
2;3-2;5	3 hours	
2;6-2;8	6 hours	
2;9-2;11	11 hours	26 sentence imitations (See Chapter 5) Question elicitation via toy telephone
3;0-3;2	12 hours	Elicitation of instruction-giving with puppets
3;3-3;5	7 hours	Bellugi's Interrogation Test
3;6-3;8	10 hours	
3;9-3;11	6 hours	
4;0-4;2	8 hours	Bellugi's Tag Question Test Ordinals Test Developmental Sentence Scoring Test Count of Mean Length of Utterance (MLU) by Morphemes
4;3-4;5	5 hours	
4;6-4;8	7 hours	Form L-M of the Stanford-Binet Intelligence Scale Peabody Picture Vocabulary Test Story Retelling Test
4;9-4;11	6 hours	Templin-Darley Tests of Articulation Berko-Gleason Morphology Test Webster-Ingram Anaphoric Pronoun Test
5;0-5;3	3 hours	
Total	101 hours	

looking at picture books and telling what she thought the story was about, and at later ages by being requested to "tell me a story about anything you'd enjoy telling about." As a rule, she responded readily either way.

While the data have not been organized in such a way as to demonstrate it, it would appear that the length and complexity of sentences, the variety of lexical items, as well as the speech registers involved vary according to the function the speech sample serves. By *function,* we refer to Halliday's 'developmental functions' (discussed further in Chapter 7) as follows:

"Instrumental	'I want'
Regulatory	'do as I tell you'
Interactional	'me and you'
Personal	'here I come'
Heuristic	'tell me why'
Imaginative	'Let's pretend'
Informative	'I've got something to tell you.' "[3]

Of these seven universal functions of language, the sample collected from Leslie appears to contain a much larger proportion of the imaginative function than samples collected by Bloom, by the Berkeley group, or by the Harvard group. This function appears to make use of more complex sentence structures and require greater variety in lexicon than the regulatory or instrumental functions, for example, which are used extensively during eating, dressing, etc. The activities the children are engaged in appear to determine to a certain extent the language functions that will be put to use, and these functions may determine certain aspects of the nature of the speech sample. The activities selected for recording also determine the speech registers most likely to be used, though these are not discussed extensively in this study; a great deal more data were collected than could be used here.

Because tape recorders were used with Leslie (by her own family and by the investigator) starting at such an early age, she has never seemed self-conscious because of the presence of one. She enjoyed listening to herself on the tape recorder, and this was her usual reward for answering questions and complying with various requests. Tape recording was the usual method of gathering data. Written transcription replaced the tape only in places where it was inconvenient to use a tape recorder, such as at an airport or a park. A notebook and pencil were kept at hand in these situations and Leslie didn't question their use. Notes regarding the tape recording sessions were sometimes made immediately following the session, but taking notes during the recording sessions at home aroused Leslie's curiosity to such an extent that she was usually distracted from the activity we were interested in. Therefore, note-taking in conjunction with tape recording was kept to a minimum.

Testing Program

One of the many purposes of language tests is to discover what a child's capabilities are without patiently waiting for the child to demonstrate them spontaneously. With Leslie, one was forced at early ages to wait until she was ready to perform a task spontaneously, because she did not perform on request. If one talked to Fred during his babbling stage, for example, he babbled in response. Leslie did not. An adult could talk to Leslie and have her full attention and apparent interest; she would smile, or perhaps laugh out loud, but would rarely babble in response. At 0;11 or 1;0, the investigator would say to Leslie, "Can you say 'mama'?" She would smile, but almost certainly would not say 'mama,' although it was in her productive repertoire at the time. In such a situation, for Fred, saying 'mama' in response seemed natural.

Many small 'tests' were tried from 2;11 to 4;6, some successfully, some not. At 2;11, for example, Leslie was playing with a toy telephone. She was pretending to talk to her cousin Gregory. In an attempt to elicit questions, the investigator suggested she ask Gregory where he had gone on his vacation; she had just finished telling about her own trip to San Diego. Other questions were suggested: ask him how he is; ask how Archie (the dog) is; ask if he went to the zoo; ask him what he's doing, etc. She not only didn't ask him any questions, she didn't initiate any conversation with him at all. After her initial /eO:O/ 'hello', she used long listening pauses and answered his questions, say 'oh,' 'me,' 'yeah,' 'uh hum,' etc.

At this same age she was given 25 sentences to repeat. The investigator asked Fred to demonstrate how it was to be done, and then she followed the instructions with ease, repeating half the sentences at one session, and the second half a week later. The sentences are listed and discussed in Chapter 5.

At 3;4 (and again, casually, several times between 3;4 and 4;2) Bellugi's Interrogation Test (Slobin[4]) was given to Leslie in another attempt to elicit questions. Leslie was particularly fond of playing with puppets, so some of her own puppets were used for this purpose. Bellugi suggests, "Using dolls or puppets, tell the child to 'Ask the doll ____,' using the indirect form of the question (e.g., "Ask the doll what she wants.") The verb phrase can be anything appropriate to the situation." Again, the testing was nonproductive. With each question suggestion from the investigator, Leslie would either look earnestly and silently at the investigator and then go on with her own conversation with the puppets, or she simply ignored the investigator's suggestion entirely.

Many reasons for her behavior may be posited. The first is that since questions were difficult for her (see Chapter 8) she did not wish to take on a difficult task. She did, however, sometimes have her dolls or puppets ask questions, but it was always a question *she* had in mind for them to ask. There is a difference between expressing someone else's meaning and expressing one's own, particularly for a child who has difficulty with speech production. A second possibility is that she may have wondered what purpose it would serve for her to ask the question. It wasn't a question she wanted an answer to. Why did anyone want her to ask it? It was typical of Leslie to want to know the reasons for doing anything. Generally, she was eager to please, so it is reasonable to assume that she must have had some reason for not doing it. The repetition of the 25 sentences mentioned above had been presented as being in the nature of a test. She had observed a few times when Fred was given language tests of various kinds and she seemed pleased to be performing a task similar to those her older brother had done. These question suggestions were not presented as a test. From her point of view, they probably represented an interference in her play.

Another possible reason for her lack of response was that she didn't understand precisely what she was to do. In reviewing the kinds of instructions she followed easily, such as "Tell me a story," and those she does not follow, such "Ask Ernie when he's coming out of the garbage can," one sees that it is general instructions that rely on her ingenuity, allow her to express her own meaning, that she follows easily. When required to do very specific things according to someone else's design, she seems less able to comply. Another example of this was her inability to understand the directions to put two triangles together to make a rectangle in performing the Stanford-Binet Intelligence Scale (discussed below).

These are possible partial explanations. However, it should be added that this non-responsiveness to verbal instructions on many occasions was a general characteristic of Leslie's. Even with such simple instructions as "Please close the door behind you," Leslie was much less likely to comply than Fred. This remains a matter for further investigation for Leslie as well as for many other children who are like her in this respect.

Bellugi's Tag Question Test (Slobin[5]) was also given to Leslie at 4;1 without success. The investigator had given this test to Fred at 3;9 and he had produced the correct tag question for more than half of the 58 sentences in the test. Many of them appeared to be very easy for him and he produced them quickly. However, when a sentence such as "I will have been swimming since this morning," for which he was unable to produce a tag, was given, he refused to try. He understood the task and produced as many as he was able to, guessing wrong on some. As with the sentence repetitions, the investigator asked Fred to demonstrate to Leslie what was meant by the instructions. It is assumed that the task was beyond her capabilities at that time rather than that she didn't understand the instructions. In Bellugi's study, Sarah had started to produce tag questions during Period D (her mean age for this period was 4;2) and Adam during Period F (mean age, 4;6).[6] As Bellugi points out, "Tag questions, then, involve an elaborate grammatical apparatus, and a certain amount of virtuosity since the shape of the tag is totally determined by the structure of the sentence and bears little semantic burden."[7] In this instance, perhaps Fred was performing in a more unusual way than Leslie.

Phonological testing for the purpose of finding out when Leslie had added certain phonemes to her productive competence were frequent. At 2;11, for example, her production of *cheese* was /kwEth/, and *jar* was /gwar/, maintaining in her substitution the voiced-voiceless feature of the initial consonant of each word. It was of interest to see, then, if she would correct both of these at one time. It was a frequent occurrence for the investigator to ask a question such as "Can you say *jar*?" Leslie usually complied good naturedly, saying the word as carefully as she could, not necessarily the way she produced it in rapid speech. Sometimes she appeared to be self-conscious about her misarticulations and would refuse to try, or sometimes she would give a silly answer and giggle. It appeared, however, that she viewed this as some kind of testing. She accepted tests. Whether or not she saw a purpose to them, they did not interfere with her play, as the instructions regarding what to say on the toy telephone or to the puppets did. It was also apparent to her that the investigator was particularly interested in her speech, and she was willing to make her progress known. She often voluntarily announced to the investigator news about what she had learned to say: "Know what? I used to say /amino/ . Now I say animal."

Formal Testing Program

During her fifth year it was determined that a battery of tests should be administered to Leslie in an attempt to compare her with other children in a variety of ways. Each of the tests given has been criticized as not being very revealing of a child's capabilities, and we do not defend any one test on this ground, but feel that in the aggregate, the tests are informative, particularly when placed side by side with the comparisons of language development of other children included in this study.

The tests decided on were (1) the Stanford-Binet Intelligence Scale (Form L-M); (2) the Peabody Picture Vocabulary Test; (3) the Developmental Sentence Scoring test designed by Lee and Canter[8] and revised by Lee and Koenigsknecht,[9] into which we have incorporated a count of the mean utterance length (MLU) as measured by morphemes; (4) a story retelling task designed by John, Horner, and Berney,[10] and administered by the investigator to Leslie and 20 other children;[11] (5) the Templin-Darley Screening and Diagnostic Tests of Articulation;[12] (6) the Berko-Gleason Morphology test;[13] and (7) a comprehension and production test of the anaphoric pronouns *he, she, him,* and *her,* developed by Webster and Ingram.[14] The results of each of these tests is discussed here.

Stanford-Binet Intelligence Scale

Intelligence tests as we know them were invented by the French psychologist Alfred Binet in 1905, and this test, which still bears his name, has been frequently revised and restandardized for use with individuals through age 18. It is the best known of all intelligence tests, and needs no further discussion here. Dr. Edith M. Dowley, Director of Bing Nursery School and Professor of Psychology and Education at Stanford University, administered the Form L-M of the Stanford-Binet to Leslie when she was 4;8. Her I.Q. on this test was 139. Dr. Dowley reported that "As revealed by this test, her greatest strengths are in visual perception, counting, reasoning, problem solving, drawing accurately and describing similarities and differences. Her weaknesses are poor immediate recall: e.g., repeating five digits and parts of stories; difficulty in defining words; and a somewhat limited background of general information. For example, she does not know the days of the week in correct order, e.g., 'Monday, Tuesday, Sunday, Friday, tomorrow'; or the meaning of 'tap,' 'roar,' and 'eyelash'; or what makes a sailboat move." She was also unable to understand the directions to put two triangles together to make a rectangle.

Dr. Dowley's final comments on Leslie were, "She is a charming little girl with a strong desire to please, a great deal of poise and self-control for her age, and truly delightful sense of humor." These findings and comments bear out the observations of the investigator in working with Leslie.

Peabody Picture Vocabulary Test (PPVT)

This test is easy to administer once one is familiar with the material, which consists of a book containing four black-and-white drawings on each page. The examiner shows the page to the child, reads a word representing one of the four pictures, and the child points to the picture that he thinks matches the word he heard. For example, on the first page there is a picture of a hairbrush, a table, a doll, and a car. They are separated by lines, and each picture is given a number from 1 to 4 so that a child could read the number instead of pointing. In our administration of the test, Leslie was instructed to point. At no time is the child required to produce a word, only to recognize the picture that represents the spoken word.

The test is designed to provide an estimate of a subject's verbal intelligence through measuring his hearing, or passive, vocabulary. The test was standardized on more than four thousand subjects in 1958 and has been widely used since then. It has proved to be especially useful with children who have difficulty responding verbally, and is designed for easy use with large numbers of children. For this reason the students used in the standardization procedure were given I.Q. tests first, and only those falling within the normal distribution (I.Q. of 85 to 115) were used in the PPVT standardization testing.

Based on a raw score of 62 correct items, Leslie's score was in the 99th percentile, according to Dunn.[15] The mean raw score for children in her group is 45.58, whereas Leslie's was 62.

Developmental Sentence Scoring (DSS)

This test (revised by Lee and Koenigsknecht[16]) is called by its authors, Lee and Canter, "a clinical procedure for estimating the status and progress of children enrolled for language training in a clinic."[17] The scoring is based on spontaneous speech samples. The procedure gives weighted scores to pronouns, verbs, negatives, conjunctions, yes-no questions, and wh-questions. The weightings are based on what the authors have found to be normal development in children; forms used by children at the earliest ages are given the lowest scores and those which are presumably more complex and learned at a later age are given a larger score. The revised weighting of 1972 was used in the scoring of Leslie's speech sample (see table 3-2.)

The test was standardized with 80 boys and 80 girls ranging in ages from 3;0 to 6;11 from middle-income, standard dialect homes, all of whom score between 85 and 115 on the Peabody Picture Vocabulary Test. The Developmental Sentence Scoring procedure is obviously of little value when used with children from nonstandard-dialect-speaking homes, and has been criticized on this count. However, Leslie does come from a middle-class, standard-dialect home, so it was considered suitable for her.

The fifty sentences used in the DSS are supposed to be complete, different, consecutive, intelligible, nonecholalic sentences elicited in conversation with an adult. Fragmentary utterances that do not constitute complete sentences are eliminated from the sample.

The authors of this procedure believe that they have selected the most critical grammatical features of a child's language for evaluation. Obviously, a procedure that considered everything would be so time-consuming to score as to be impractical. The eight features considered are: (1) indefinite pronouns and/or noun modifiers, (2) personal pronouns, (3) main verbs, (4) secondary verbs, (5) negatives, (6) conjunctions, (7) interrogative reversals, and (8) wh-questions. In order to partially compensate for other features not considered, an additional sentence point is added to the total sentence score if the entire sentence is correct in all respects (adult, standard dialect English).

The fifty consecutive sentences produced by Leslie at 4;1 which were used for the DSS scoring, along with the scores, are shown in table 3-2. Leslie's DSS score of 9.98 puts her over the 90th percentile of children her age, as tested and scored by Lee and Koenigsknecht,[18] Children of Leslie's age in the 50th percentile had scores of 7.5.

One of the features of the DSS that should be pointed out is that it gives points for what is done 'right,' but no points are ever deducted for what is done 'wrong.' It is assumed that if a child makes many 'mistakes' he will simply have a lower score than the children who don't. The DSS score tells us only that Leslie's sentences are longer and/or more complex than those of most other children tested by this method. Another child might have the same score that Leslie has and have a grammar that coincides well with the adult grammar—every sentence might have been "correct in all respects." This scoring method is not sensitive to that difference. This is not being pointed out by way of criticism of the scoring system, but to point out that qualitatively,

Table 3-2
Developmental Sentence Scoring

Fifty Consecutive Sentences Produced by Leslie (4;1) in Conversation with her Brother, Fred, and the Investigator

		1	2	3	4	5	6	7	8	9	10	11
		Indefinite Pronoun	Personal Pronoun	Main Verb	Secondary Verb	Negative	Conjunction	Interrogative Reversal	Wh Question	Sentence Point	Total	# Morphemes
1.	From a clothes, I mean, cause it's going a rain.	1	1	1,1	2					0	6	11
2.	Sparks never do anything.	7	1	1						1	9	5
3.	A rain coming from a cloud. (Rain comes from a cloud.)			0						0	0	7
4.	Know how little this is?	1		1,1	0		8			0	11	5
5.	I talking in here (microphone).		1	0						0	1	5
6.	When I was uh. . .one uh. . .I didn't know what to do so I cried and cried and I played a little song with my trumpet.		1,1 1,1 1	2,4 2,2 2	3	7	8,8 5,3 3			1	55	29
7.	I didn't know where my trumpet was.		1,1	4,2		7	8			1	24	8
8.	I was finding it my crib.	1	1,1	1						0	4	8
9.	I was looking everywhere for it.	1	1	1						1	4	8
10.	Then I saw some buttons on my trumpet.	3	1,1	2						1	8	10
11.	You know what I call my trumpet? (trumpet)		1,1	1,1			8			1	13	7
12.	Does this work anymore?			4				6		1	12	4
13.	I got a pen like this.	1	1	1			8			0	11	6
14.	I can't find it any more.	1,3	1	4		4				1	14	7
15.	Does this write?	1		4				6		1	12	3
16.	/du/ try purple. (I'll try purple.)									0	0	3
17.	When I was one I find I was two.		1,1 1	2,2 1			8			1	17	11
18.	Yes, I was /fɪn/. (fighting)		1	2						1	4	5

Table 3-2 (continued)

	1	2	3	4	5	6	7	8	9	10	11
19. No, I was /fIning/. (fighting)		1	2						1	4	6
20. Because I didn't like anybody.	7	1	4			6			1	19	6
21. Now I do.			1						1	3	3
22. Then I was looking like monster. . .like with my hands like that (demonstrates) cause I used to be saying, well, that looks like a monster.	1, 1	1,1, 1	2, 1	7		6		8	0	23	27
23. Way you. . . which way do you go?		1	4						1	14	5
24. Any kind what you like, we like too.	1	1,3	1,1						0	7	8
25. I want to do that one. (go to that one)	1	1	1	5					1	9	6
26. I never /bEd/ (be + ed) at that one before.	1	1	0						0	2	8
27. I like this is a /pomus. .hipomus/. (hippopotamus)	1	1	1,1						0	4	6
28. It /rUry/ (really) is.	1	1	1						1	3	3
29. Well, sparks are kinda little and /ist/ (just) climb and don't have any feet. . .no arms and feet, eyes and nose and mouth, no mouth and no head.	7,3; 3; 3	1	1; 1,4		4	3; 3,3,3			1	43	31
30. Know what sparks are?								2	1	4	5
31. Most sparks are little, some are kinds oozed from. . .from lions new things like a donut. . . and it comes from lamps.	3		1; 1,4			3				12	27
32. From parties. . .no. . .from ummmm. . .maybe roofs, I think.		1	1			3			0	2	9
33. Shoot out!		1	1						1	2	2
34. Know what?									1	1	2

	1	2	3	4	5	6	7	8	9	10	11
35. I uh kind a know when I was a (at the) doctor's		1,1	1,2						0	41	43
and uh I didn't like have my shot and one guy	3	1,1									
put it on my...in my...one a (of the) /gUrz/	1,3		2	0	4	8,3					
(girls) put it in my arm and I let out a scream.	1	1									
36. Hippo on that program, know what? Say hi, hi, hi	1		2,2			3			0	2	10
37. And he is wrong.			1,0						1	7	4
38. I need lunch first!	7	2	1						1	10	4
39. I going get something yummy.	3	1	1			3			0	4	6
40. That work.	1		0						0	1	2
41. These one don't.	0		0						0	4	4
42. It's kind of square. (Description of tape recorder.)	1		0	4					1	3	5
43. It's a like that.	1,1		1						0	3	5
44. No, that one are look like. (It doesn't look like that.)	1,3		0						0	4	6
45. See like Fred /dUez/ (do + s).			1,0						0	1	5
46. That's how our table /gOd/ (go + d).	1	3	1,0			8			0	13	7
47. Want to see how rings xxx...like I do in bed.	1	1	1	5		8			0	15	11
48. Well, I /est/ (just) lay quiet and I lay straight	1,1	1,1	1,1			3			1	8	9
49. That's how ours lay. (Their tape recorder does	1	3	1,0			8			0	13	5
not sit on edge, it lays flat.)											
50. I didn't choose yet.	1	4		7					1	13	5

Total points on sentence scoring—499
Total morphemes—427
DSS = 9.98 (499 divided by 50, the number of sentences)
MLU = 8.54 (427 divided by 50, the number of sentences)

we believe that Leslie's sentences are more complex, but further removed from adult standard English than those of most other children, though the DSS does not indicate this. We will see on Leslie's score on the story retelling tasks, discussed below, that she did, in fact, produce more grammatical immaturities than the other children in that study.

We did not have more detailed information regarding the scoring of the children by Lee and Koenigsknecht so that we could compare Leslie on each of the eight grammatical feature groups plus the sentence points. This might have told us something of her comparative strengths and weaknesses.

Using this same sample of 50 sentences (taken when Leslie was 4;1), we have calculated her mean length of utterance (MLU) using the standard method of counting morphemes.[19] Again, the MLU is not very revealing of a child's language ability, but it is a measure that has been widely used and so offers some means of comparison. This was not considered to be practical at earlier stages in Leslie's development, however, because of the difficulty in interpreting her utterances. Standard procedure requires (reasonably enough) that a word (or morpheme) must be glossed in order to be counted, and at earlier ages, so much of Leslie's speech samples had to be eliminated on this basis as to give a warped picture. At an age when other children were using long intelligible sentences, Leslie was using longer unintelligible sentences, but just as other children knew what they were saying, Leslie appeared to know what she was saying. The fact that the investigator (as well as her parents) did not know what she was saying should not be counted against her in measuring the length of her sentences.

As can be seen from table 3-2, Leslie's MLU at 4;1 was 8.54, as calculated from this sample. At 4.2 Adam's MLU was 5.15 and Sarah's was 4.0.[20] Eve was no longer being studied at this age.

Story Retelling Task

We have borrowed, in large part, the methods used by John, Horner, and Berney[21] in having Leslie and twenty other children, eleven of whom were Yakima Indian children, retell the story *Curious George.*[22] (See Weeks and Weeks[23].) John et al. examined the retold stories as "patterned verbal output." They were considering at least two types of patterning (p. 251): linguistic and cognitive. Children transform the story into their own words, reflecting their level of syntactic and vocabulary development (linguistic patterning). In addition, they selectively recall features of the original story and impose their own organization on them (cognitive patterning). The two principal indices of these types of patterning are what they call "stimulus-derived" (SD) phrases and "story-relevant inferred" (SRI) phrases (a phrase being a subject-predicate construction in most instances). Both kinds of phrases are based on the text of the story, as opposed to phrases the child makes up on the basis of the story illustrations or his own imagination, but the SD phrases are those based on something shown in the illustration whereas the SRI phrases are not illustrated in any way. For example, when the text says "The man in the yellow hat saw George," and shows a picture illustrating this, and the child repeats something to this effect, e.g., "The man saw George," this is considered an SD phrase. If the text says "George was curious," but does not illustrate it, and the child repeats it, it would be an SRI phrase. In fact, this is one of the many examples of text material that couldn't be illustrated, at least in any simple way. Dialogue is another example.

John et al. hypothesized that the production by the child of SRI phrases is a more demanding cognitive task than the production of the more directly cued SD phrases. They also found that the production of SRI phrases correlated significantly with performance on the Peabody Picture Vocabulary Test, which was given to half of their 142 subjects.[24] While there undoubtedly were some differences in our handling of the method and theirs, our results seem comparable. For example, we have calculated from John et al.'s study[25] of 60 black children a weighted mean[a] of 69.5 total phrases produced, with a standard deviation of 22.2. In our study, the children produced an average of 70.8 phrases, and the standard deviation was 19.3 A second measure which we were able to compare showed the same closeness-of-fit. From John et al.'s data, we calculated that the mean number of relevant (i.e., SD or SRI) phrases per 10 total phrases produced by the children was 6.3 whereas the children in our sample produced 6.7 relevant phrases per 10 phrases of any type. These comparisons suggest that we were consistently measuring the same selected aspects of a child's linguistic and cognitive skills.

We added two measures, which we called *grammatical immaturities* and *intactness*. We counted as grammatical immaturities such non-adult forms as regularized verbs (*holded*), non-adult plurals (*foots*), non-adult comparatives (*upper* to mean *higher*), incorrect verb tense or nonagreement of verb and noun ("*He catch* him in a bag"), non-agreement of noun and pronoun in gender or number (*all that fish*), and omission of essential words ("How come they ___ hanging?"). Each immature form received a score of one, and no one immaturity was counted more than once. (See Weeks and Weeks[26] for phrase production data.) Leslie produced the largest number of grammatical immaturities of any of the children tested, averaging about one immaturity for every four phrases produced. The boy who ranked second on this measure and produced about one immaturity for every seven phrases produced was from a Spanish/English bilingual home.

Only one child, other than Fred (who was not included in the statistical analysis of this study), produced no grammatical immaturities at all.

---

[a]In John's study, means were reported separately by social class, and thus, a weighted mean for the entire sample had to be calculated.

By *intactness* we were referring to a child's production of phrases, which were not necessarily verbatim, but which were so similar as to give the impression that the child had, in fact, recalled the phrases of the text and was trying to reproduce it rather than having reorganized the material in an original way. Approximately three-fourths of a phrase had to be the same, and this three-fourths had to include the verb and the noun or a suitable pronoun (or vice versa). Adjectives could be deleted and prepositions changed, for example. Grammatical immaturities which were substituted for adult forms did not detract from the intactness of a phrase

This was one of the measures which particularly interested us where Leslie was concerned because, as mentioned earlier in connection with her Stanford-Binet evaluation, one of her weaknesses was short-term memory—a fact which the investigator had noticed on many occasions. The story retelling task did not directly involve short-term memory, which is usually thought of as involving a time span of perhaps one to twenty seconds. It involved long-term memory or intermediate-term memory, if one adopts Wickelgren's[27] definition as that which has a time constant in the range from two minutes to several hours. Now, if one lacks in short-term memory skills, how does one bypass this to reproduce phrases intact?

In our day-to-day contact with Leslie, this had seemed to be the sort of task—reproducing phrases in the same form in which she heard them—that she was least skilled in. Perhaps it was unfortunate that she had always been compared with her cousin John and with Fred, both of whom are particularly adept at this. In the story retelling task, Fred produced 32 intact phrases and John produced 25, all of which were produced from seventh illustration on. Up to that point, John had been so upset with himself for not being able to produce the entire book verbatim that he hadn't really applied himself to the task. It had always been the case that John had enjoyed repeating adult-sounding phrases he had heard and apparently made a conscious effort to remember them. For example, the investigator had once taken him shopping (at 3;8) for an item his mother wanted. We were unsuccessful, and on the way home, the investigator said "I'm really sorry we couldn't find what your mother wanted." John thought about it momentarily, then said "I'm going to say that to Mommy." He often used phrases he had heard, but this was the first time we had heard him express this intention. He would say such things as "Indeed not!" in imitation of his father. Often it was his repeating a phrase incorrectly that called it to attention: "I want to tell you something before I think of it," (4;2), meaning *before I forget it*; and "Well, not in this instant," (5;8), meaning *not in this instance*. Likewise, at 2;5 Fred asked as we were outdoors on a March morning, "It's chilly today, isn't it?" and at 3;1, when asked what he wanted for Chirstmas, he replied "My concern is about toys."

Through her sixth year Leslie was never heard using such 'borrowed' phrases in spontaneous speech situations. However, in the story retelling task she produced eleven intact phrases, which ranked her fifth, along with two other children (one of whom was the youngest child tested—a Yakima boy). This suggests that she did have this capability in a situation where she interpreted it as being required. Perhaps her failure to use borrowed phrases in spontaneous speech was due, at least in part, to a lack of desire or interest in it.

It is of interest to note that our results indicated that while the production of SD phrases and SRI phrases both show a substantial correlation with age, the production of intact phrases does not. The production of intact phrases was unrelated to all characteristics measured in the story retelling task except the production of SRI phrases ($r = .59$), suggesting that this may be an aspect of cognitive patterning, involving some special memory skill.

Leslie compares with the other children in the story retelling task as follows: she had the highest number of grammatical immaturities of any of the children, producing .2363 immaturities per phrase where the mean was .08; on the measure of accuracy (the ratio of SD and SRI phrases to total phrases produced) she ranked next to the bottom, scoring .4909 where the mean was .67. The lowest ranking child was also the youngest, a Yakima boy, who also produced eleven intact phrases. He produced a total of 115 phrases and Leslie produced 110, while the mean was 71. Many of this Yakima boy's and Leslie's phrases were irrelevant; they both did what John et al. termed "embroidering" the story. Again, in their terminology, these two children were the most "verbal." Leslie produced 44 SD phrases, where 35 was the mean, and she produced 10 SRI phrases, where 10.9 was the mean. In view of the fact that she was among the younger children tested (four younger than she, sixteen older), the SD, SRI and intact phrase scores were comparatively high.

The Templin-Darley Tests of Articulation

This is another test which had been validated with large numbers of children and is widely used. The test includes 176 items, 50 of which constitute a screening test. When the test is used at school, it is the screening test that determines which children need speech correction because their articulation is inadequate for their age. The remainder of the test is for use in a finer evaluation of the child's articulation problems.

The test is easy to administer. There are 57 cards, each with 2 to 4 pictures per card. The examiner points to the picture he is referring to and reads a "starter" sentence that is designed to elicit the appropriate word from the child. For example, on one card is a picture of an Indian boy using a bow and arrow, and the examiner reads "He's shooting a bow and _____ ." The child is supposed to say "arrow."

Leslie experienced some difficulty in producing all of the words spontaneously.

The first item, for example, is a picture of two bare feet. The examiner read, "You have two _____ ," and Leslie said "foots." The item was for the purpose of eliciting an /E/. The manual suggests that the child be told that you have some drawings and that you want him to tell you what each is a picture of. Then it suggests that if the child does not produce the word spontaneously (with or without the prompting of the sentence) the examiner say the word for him and ask him to repeat it. The problem was that Leslie assumed this was a test in which she was supposed to know the answers, and when the examiner had to say it for her and have her repeat it, she thought she had failed. She said about three-fourths of the way through, "This is hard!"

The test results indicated, however, that her articulation was clearly adequate. Her score on the screening test was 48: she misarticulated only *yellow* (she said *lellow*), and in *shredded* of shredded wheat, she substituted /sw/ for /shr/. However, both of these items were among those she had to be asked to repeat after the examiner. She said a sunflower was orange (rather than yellow) and she was completely unfamiliar with shredded wheat as a breakfast cereal and so produced nothing for that item until told. This caused her some embarrassment, which resulted as usual in a softer voice and less careful articulation (see Chapter 2 for a discussion of such speech registers).

The mean score for girls 5 years old (Leslie was 4;9 when tested) is 40.6 correct out of the 50, and the cut-off score which separates adequate from inadequate performance at this age is 30.[28] Results on this test indicate that Leslie had made great strides in the area of articulation, for as mentioned earlier in this chapter, she was extremely difficult to understand at earlier ages. But, as will be discussed in Chapter 4, she was also very diligent in working to improve her articulation.

A possibility that should be considered is that there is a greater difference between Leslie's careful articulation, such as on this test, and that which Labov's subjects displayed when reading word lists,[29] or in rapid speech, than is usually the case. We have not attempted to compare her with other children in this regard.

Berko-Gleason Morphology Test

This is not a standardized test in the sense that the Peabody Picture Vocabulary Test or the Stanford-Binet are, but it is an ingenious method devised by Berko-Gleason to test children's productive knowledge of English morphology by eliciting various inflections, derivations, and compounds.[30] Nonsense words and original line drawings are used, e.g., the experimenter shows the child a picture of a strange looking bird-like creature, and below it, two identical creatures, and says, "This is a wug. Now there is another one. There are two of them. There are two _____ ." The child is supposed to say "wugs." There are 27 picture cards and questions for which the child produces an answer.

In her original study Berko-Gleason tested 56 children ranging from four to seven years of age. Leslie's answers have been compared with those of the preschoolers tested by Berko-Gleason. While Leslie compared favorably, she did not follow closely in producing only those answers that a majority of other preschoolers produced and missing those that they missed. On the past tense forms she produced *spowed* and *motted* along with only 36 percent and 32 percent respectively of the other preschoolers, while she missed *binged* and *glinged,* which 60 percent and 63 percent respectively of Berko-Gleason's preschoolers produced correctly. It is unknown why *bing* and *gling* confused her, but she asked for both of them to be repeated before she answered incorrectly.

We hesitatingly gave Leslie credit for *reng* where *rang* was required because she didn't recognize the word herself when she heard it later on the tape, out of context. However, all of her vowels typically have a wide range.

Conducted before the days of cassette recorders, Berko-Gleason's 1958 study was done without this linguistic aid. We discovered two plurals, both dental fricatives (th) rather than sibilants (s or z), which were so faint as to be imperceptible during testing, but definitely noticeable upon careful listening to the tape. This test makes no requirement that the plural be enunciated in an adult fashion, only that it be of the adult form.

The Webster-Ingram Anaphoric Pronoun Test

This test was designed at the Institute for Childhood Aphasia at Stanford University for use principally with linguistically deviant children,[31] but was used by Webster and Ingram with both normal and deviant children. It consists of two parts: a comprehension test and a production test of the pronouns *she, her, he,* and *him.* It is carried out with a family of small dolls, a mother, a father, a boy, and a girl. The dolls are soft plastic and their arms and legs can be easily moved. The comprehension task consists of the examiner letting the child manipulate the dolls while the examiner says what they are doing, e.g., the examiner says, "The girl kisses the boy and now she is patting him," and the child is expected to move the dolls in such a way that they appear to be doing this. The production task consists of having the child explain what the dolls are doing when the examiner manipulates them.

Webster and Ingram tested 60 subjects, 30 of whom were considered normal in their language acquisition and 30 of whom were linquistically deviant. The normal group ranged in age from 3;0 to 4;5. At the time of testing, Leslie was 4;9, four months older than the oldest children in the test group. The oldest subjects in the normal group produced between 88 percent and 97 percent correct responses on the comprehension task. On the production task, 5 normal subjects used the pronouns correctly. None of the children in the deviant sample had established the use of all four of the pronouns under study with any degree of stability.

Leslie made no errors whatsoever in the comprehension or production of the pronouns.

Notes

1. Lois Bloom, *Language development: Form and function in emerging grammars* (Cambridge, Mass.: M.I.T. Press, 1970), p. 16.
2. Thelma E. Weeks, "Speech registers in young children," *Child Development,* 1971, 42:1119–31.
3. M.A.K. Halliday, "Relevant models of language," in *Explorations in the functions of language* (London: Edward Arnold, 1973).
4. Dan I. Slobin (ed.), "A field manual for cross-cultural study of the acquisition of communicative competence," multilithed report, University of California, Berkeley, 1967.
5. Ibid., p. 203-5.
6. Ursula Bellugi, "The acquisition of negation," unpublished Ph.D. dissertation, Harvard University, 1967.
7. Ibid., p. 157.
8. Laura L. Lee, and Susan M. Canter, "Developmental sentence scoring: a clinical procedure for estimating syntactic development in children's spontaneous speech," *Journal of Speech and Hearing Disorders,* 1971, 36:315-40.
9. Laura L. Lee, and Roy A. Koenigsknecht, "Developmental sentence scoring (revised)," Northwestern University, 1972.
10. Vera P. John, Vivian M. Horner, and Tomi D. Berney, "Story retelling: a study of sequential speech in young children," in *Basic studies on reading,* edited by H. Levin and J.P. Williams (New York: Basic Books, 1970), pp. 246-62.
11. Thelma E. Weeks, and John R. Weeks, "Some measures of the relation between linguistic and cognitive skills in young Yakima Indian and non-Indian children," unpublished paper, Stanford University, 1973.
12. Mildred C. Templin, and Frederic L. Darley, *The Templin-Darley Tests of Articulation* (Iowa: Bureau of Educational Research and Service, University of Iowa, 1960).
13. Jean Berko-Gleason, "The child's learning of English morphology," *Word,* 1958, 14:150-77.
14. Brendan O. Webster, and David Ingram, "The comprehension and production of the anaphoric pronouns 'he, she, him, her' in normal and linquistically deviant children," *Papers and reports on child language development,* Stanford University, 1972, 4:55-77.
15. Lloyd M. Dunn, *Expanded manual for the Peabody Picture Vocabulary Test* (Minnesota: American Guidance Service, Inc., 1965), p. 20, table 5.

16. Lee and Koenigsknecht, "Developmental sentence scoring (revised)."
17. Lee and Canter, "Developmental sentence scoring."
18. Lee and Koenigsknecht, "Developmental sentence scoring (revised)."
19. Dan I. Slobin, "A field manual for cross-cultural study," pp. 19-20.
20. Roger Brown, Courtney Cazden, and Ursula Bellugi-Klima, "The child's grammar from I to III," *Minnesota Symposia on Child Psychology,* vol. II, edited by J.P. Hill (Minneapolis: University of Minnesota Press, 1968), pp. 28-73.
21. John, Horner, and Berney, "Story retelling."
22. H.A. Rey, *Curious George* (Boston: Houghton-Mifflin, 1941).
23. Weeks, and Weeks, "Some measures of the relation between linguistic and cognitive skills,"
24. Vera John, and Tomi D. Berney, "Analysis of story retelling as a measure of the effects of ethnic content in stories," Final report, Office of Economic Opportunity, Project No. 577, 1967.
25. John et al., "Story retelling."
26. Weeks, and Weeks, "Some measures of the relation between linguistic and cognitive skills."
27. Wayne A. Wickelgren, "Coding, retrieval, and dynamics of multitrace associative memory," *Cognition in learning and memory*, edited by Lee W. Gregg (New York: Wiley, 1972), pp. 19-50.
28. Templin, and Darley, *The Templin-Darley Tests of Articulation*, p. 19.
29. William Labov, *Social stratification of English in New York City* (Washington: Center for Applied Linguistics, 1966).
30. Jean Berko-Gleason, "The child's learning of English morphology," *Word,* 1958, 14:150-77.
31. Webster, and Ingram, "The comprehension and production of the anaphoric pronouns."

4 Phonological Development

The aspect of language acquisition that afforded Leslie the most difficulty from the point of view of the investigator, Leslie's family, and, from all indications, Leslie herself, was the acquisition of the phonological system. This chapter will discuss the following aspects of Leslie's acquisition of phonology: (1) Leslie's preference for velars, (2) her use of consonant harmony within a reduplicated-syllable word pattern, (3) her reliance on vowels to function as words, and (4) her own awareness of her difficulty in acquiring the phonological system of English.

Velar Preference

Jakobson hypothesized that dentals are the 'unmarked' consonant, and that if the model contains consonants which are not yet in the child's repertoire, he may substitute a dental for them.[1] Leslie appeared to follow this rule in some instances. In the example below a specification is made as to whether the consonant or consonant cluster involved is present or absent in that position in her productive competence.

> /dedE/ 'Reggie' (the dog) Neither the /r/ of the stressed
> syllable nor the /j/ of the unstressed one had yet been
> acquired by Leslie. (1;5)
>
> /dUdUtwA/ 'choo choo train' /ch/ not yet acquired. (2;10)
>
> /depE/ 'empty' Words with initial vowels were difficult for
> Leslie; there are a number of instances where she added an
> initial consonant (discussed below). (3;2)

In other instances, however, Leslie did not proceed according to Jakobson's expectations nor follow the usual pattern of acquisition of consonants. Jakobson argues for the fact that velars develop after dentals, and often dentals substitute for the velars until a child's sixth year, e.g., /tut/ for *cut*. Leslie acquired velars among her first consonants. As mentioned in Chapter 2, Leslie's first monoremes were: /dada/ 'daddy,' /momo/ 'mommy,' /gogo/ 'doggie,' /baba/ 'pattycake,' and /gaga/, an expression of happiness.

There are numerous reports of children using a velar or velar fricatives for a happy sound, such as Leslie's /gaga/, at a prelinguistic or beginning linguistic stage, but not actually adding the velar to their phonemic inventory until a later age. Jakobson says, "Thus in children who do not yet have any velar phonemes, one observes *gi* as an imitation of falling blinds, *kra kra* of the raven's cawing, *gaga* as an indication of pleasure . . .".[2] Lewis also mentions the velar as a sound expressing happiness or satiety.[3] Leslie's cousin Gregory also used the velar /gEgE/ as an expression of pleasure.

Leslie's velar, however, was a permanent part of her phonemic inventory. While she dropped /gaga/ from her lexicon within a short time after 1;0, she did not drop /gogo/. On the contrary, she dropped /dada/ and for more than a year used /gogE/ as a name for both her father and the dog.

Most children seem to add the velar to their phonemic inventory at a time later than 0;11. Lewis indicates on a chart that Hilde Stern added both the /k/ and /g/ at 1;4; Deville's daughter added the /g/ at 1;4; and K (the child studied by Lewis) added it at 1;6.[4] Fudge reports that his son added it at 1;4.[5] At this point his son not only used /gugU/ for *doggie*, but /kEgE/ for *piggie,* and at 1;5 added /gink/ for *sink*.

Leslie seemed to have an even stronger preference for velars than the children whose speech development has been looked at in this study. This can be seen in examples from her first monoremes to a time quite late in her speech development; many examples will be seen below. Further research on the favored places of articulation of children who are slow in speech development may be indicated.

Consonant Harmony

In Leslie's first words both the vowel and the consonant of the first syllable were reduplicated in the second. Within a short time her words took on more diverse patterns, but she retained a strong tendency toward consonant harmony in two-syllable words. Voicing did not necessarily match, however. Late in her speech development she was still using partial consonant harmony:

/trumpənt/ 'trumpet' (4;1)

/slanə/ Claus 'Santa Claus' (3;7)

/kloklit/ 'chocolate' (3;7)

Syllables appeared to be counted, and a word perceived as two syllables would be produced as a reduplication of one syllable or the other, depending on a number of factors, such as stress, recency, features included in the syllable model, and features that have been acquired by the child at that point.

Consonant harmony may evolve in three ways: both consonants may differ from those of the model, both consonants may match that of the second syllable of the model (anticipatory assimilation), or both consonants may match that of the first syllable of the model (persevering assimilation). As will be seen from the above examples, one element of a consonant cluster was chosen for reduplication.

Leopold defines *assimilation* as the unconscious modification of the articulation of a sound, [6] which makes it more similar to that of a neighboring sound, the result being an economy of articulatory effort. He rejects the common terms *progressive* and *regressive* assimilation as being hopelessly confused, and instead uses *anticipatory* for cases in which the articulation of the first sound is modified by anticipation of that of the second sound, and *persevering* for cases in which the second sound is modified by a lingering of the articulation of the first. Assimilation, he adds, usually affects two sounds in contact, but "assimilation at a distance" frequently occurs in child language also. Leslie's consonant harmony involves assimilation at a distance. Leopold says that anticipatory assimilation is far more frequent than persevering, and this was true of Leslie's assimilations.

Examples of Leslie's consonant harmony follow, first those involving anticipatory assimilation, then persevering, then examples in which both consonants differ. Again, in each case a specification is made as to whether the consonant or consonant cluster involved is present or absent in that position in her productive competence.

Anticipatory Assimilation:

/gogo/ 'doggie' /d/ present (0;11)

/ngongə/ 'book' (modeled after *song* book) /s/ not present (1;6)

/gugO/ 'freckle' /fr/ not present (2;6)

/bUbuth/ 'schoolbus' /sk/ not present (2;7)

/hEhar/ 'sweetheart' /sw/ not present (in *sweater*, /f/ was used as a substitute) (2;9)

/popo/~/bopo/ 'grandpa' /gr/ not present (2;9)

/bAbE beOth/ 'jingle bells' (perhaps '*baby* bells') /j/ not present, /g/ present (2;9)

/gikE/ 'Mickey' (Mouse) /m/ present (2;10)

/gungkn/ 'pumpkin' /p/ present (2;10)

/gakUm/ 'racoon' /r/ present (2;10)

/ratit/ 'rabbit' /b/ present (2;10)

/gEkIn/ 'this kind' /th/ not present (2;10)

/gokO/ 'taco' /t/ present (2;10)

/bopm/ 'apple' Another example of her supplying an initial
consonant to make a word easier for her to articulate. /1/
not present (2;10)

/biprz/ 'slippers' /sl/ not present (2;10)

/twEtwEtwE/ 'Christmas tree' /kr/,/sm/ not present (2;10)
(A good replica of *Christmas tree* was beyond Hildegard's
capability, too. Leopold reported that she used the form
/dzidzitE/.)

/wauwr/ 'flower' /fl/ not present (2;10)

/gupə/ 'puppet' /p/ present (2;11)

Persevering Assimilation:

/nOnO/ 'window' /w/, /d/ present (2;6)

/bubO/ 'bottle' /t/ present (2;7) (*Baby bottle* was /bEbobO/
at this age, and /bAbE boO/ at 2;10.)

/bupO/ 'pencil' /s/ not present (2;10)

/bobE/ 'body' /d/ present (2;10)

/gEgE gogə/ 'cookie monster' (on Sesame Street) /m/ present,
/nst/ not present (2;10)

/hahr/ 'hammer' /m/ present (2;10)

/hehE/ 'heavy' /v/ not present in medial position (2;10)
Previously she had used the form /eE/.

/mimi/ 'minute' /n/ present (2;10)

Both Consonants Represent Substitutes:

/dedE/ 'Reggie' /r/, /j/ not present (1;5)

/gEgE/ 'baby' /b/ present (1;5)

/gogo/ 'dollie' /d/ present /l/ not present (1;7)

/wuwA/ 'airplane' /pl/ not present. Another example of her
supplying an initial consonant. (2;4)

/babin/ 'wagon' /w/, /g/ present (2;6) The velar does not
assimilate the /w/ here, perhaps because the velar is voiced.
Note in the examples of anticipatory assimilation that, with the
exception of *doggie,* all examples with velars have models with
voiceless *k.*

/wewe/ 'sweater' (or blanket or sleepers) /sw/ not present
/t/ is present, but we have no examples in Leslie's phonology
where this medial flap, such as in *sweater,* is realized in initial
position as a dental. That is, /dede/ would seem to be a
possibility, but such examples do not occur in her speech.

/fefr/ 'sweater' /sw/ not present (2;10) At this same age,
Hildegard used the form /fetr/ for *sweater.*

/fefn/~/fefe/ 'blanket or sleepers' Still modeled after *sweater,*
but she now differentiates by the final segment. (2;10)

/vEvEz/ 'Beezie' (a toy clown) /b/ present, /z/ not present
in medial position (2;11)

It can be seen that the substitutions listed above involve consonants or
consonant clusters not yet within Leslie's productive competence about half
of the time. The other half of the time, then, it should theoretically have
been possible for her to use the consonant in the model, but she did not.

Smith,[7] whose son also had a velar preference and employed velars in
a consonant harmony rule, maintains that every child seems to have some
variant of a consonant harmony rule. The difference between children, then,
lies in the extent to which a child uses such a rule at an early age, and the length
of time that the child continues to use it.

Reliance on Vowels

While Leslie had difficulty with vowel-initial words during the early stages of her speech development, she had no difficulty with vowels in isolation; she used them abundantly. There seemed to be some way in which either the word pattern V or CVC were easier for Leslie than VC. As mentioned earlier, it was often the case that she modified VC words to CVC. We have no ready explanation for this.

In view of Leslie's difficulty with consonant production, it is not surprising that many of Leslie's words consisted of vowels without consonants. Some of these could be glossed and some could not. The /E/~/A/ functor referred to in Chapter 5 is an example of a use that cannot be explicitly glossed. There were instances, however, where the /E/ represented a particular word, such as *Winnie*, in Winnie the Pooh:

/E pU ber/ 'Winnie Pooh Bear' (2;11)

Also, *ladybug* was consistently /E beg/. In both of these cases, the final phoneme of the word is used to represent the entire word, although this is not the stressed vowel. In these cases the vowel is quite accurately represented. In many cases, this was not true. In the following instance, the /O/ does not represent accurately the vowel of *love*:

/A O mE/ 'They love me.' (3;0)

For a short time around 2;7 Leslie called her brother Fred /e/. The cluster *fr* was not within her productive competence at that time. The *d* was within her productive competence, but only in initial position; she had no final stop consonants at this time. This would have precluded the possibility of /ed/ as a name for Fred. A further difficulty was in the VC shape, which she did not usually produce at this age (e.g., *open* was /pO/). Leslie did not seem to think that a vowel without any consonant was an appropriate name for Fred. She experimented with /ha/, but this bore no great similarity to his name, and she reverted to calling him *boy*.

Other examples of vowels used as words:

/AO/ 'yellow' (2;10)

/A Oi/ 'They're toys.' (2;6)

/E o/ 'green car' (2;6)

/U E o/ '(?)' (2;6)

/aO/ 'owl' (2;10)

/a E fE/ 'hand in way' (Your hand's in the way.) (2;11)

/E A u bE...dE.../ '(?)' (2;11)

/eO:O/ 'hello' (3;0)

Few examples of this are found after about 3;6, at which time most words had at least one consonant.

An additional problem in understanding Leslie was that there was great variation in the vowel quality, both in words she knew well and in new lexical items.

Leslie's Awareness of Her Phonological Problems

In almost every respect Leslie seemed to acquire language more slowly and with more difficulty than Fred, and she herself seemed to view at least the speech production aspects of language acquisition as difficult. For example, at 2;10 she was asked to name the animals in a puzzle she had just put together easily. When she came to the elephant she said /ə tOm/ rather softly as though she were uncertain about the word. When asked to repeat it she said,

/I ka a E hard/ 'I can't. That is hard!' (2;10)

At 2;11, when asked to repeat a compound sentence with two unrelated clauses, she was unable to repeat the second clause (see page 71, Chapter 5) and said "Ohh . . . . .". She was crushed by her own failure. And often, after practicing a difficult word three or four times at her own instigation and still not articulating it correctly, she would pause and sigh a long sigh. She repeatedly demonstrated her awareness of her inability to cope with speech production.

Target Words

One of Leslie's strategies for simplifying her task seemed to be to select target words for practice. For example, at 2;7 she was referring to a dress and called it /ə yeth/. Not being quite certain what she was saying, the investigator asked "A dress?" and Leslie repeated it three times, trying with each attempt to improve it:

/defth...deth...dwesh/ 'dress' (2;7)

It may be noted that after hearing the model, she included the initial consonant correctly on each attempt. Her memory of the vowel had been accurate, but memory of the consonants apparently was not. There are many examples that indicate that there was a processing and/or storage problem rather (or in addition to) a production problem, e.g.,

> Know what? This time we going to play a different gray.
> (game)　(4;2)

We can see here that *game* did not offer a production problem, only a storage problem. In the case of *dress*, the initial consonant cluster presented a problem to the extent that *dr* was not in her productive repertoire. It has been suggested that Leslie may have analyzed this cluster as a unit, and that *y* was her substitution for the entire unit. However, her more accurate production of *d* or *dw* for the cluster, after hearing it said, suggests again that it was a storage problem. This was her first recorded use of *dress,* and there are no examples of her use of other items modeled after words with an initial *dr* cluster, so we have no clear evidence regarding her analysis of this cluster.

The following sample of target words she worked on during the two-month period of 2;10 to 3;0, however, did present production problems:

Gregory	shoes
Fred	dress
Hopper (Mrs. Hopper)	moon
grasshopper	chair
rabbit	butterfly
part	pig
apart	things
in a minute (used as a word)	squirrel
box	bottle
letters of the alphabet:　x, h, w	
numbers:　six, seven	

Leslie drilled herself on these words much as a student learning a second language might. There was some particular aspect of each word that she appeared to be working on (she did her own 'programming'). For example, just previous to 2;10, she had been working at the task of adding a final /k/ to words requiring it. *Milk*, which has been /br/, became /mrk/ at the same that she added *quick,* pronounced perfectly, to her lexicon. However, she had not yet mastered the voiced velar in final position: *pig* was /pEn/, *big* was /bEn/. She was aware of her misarticulation, and was working on it.

One of her strategies for articulating a second consonant in a word was to carry a phonological feature from the first consonant to the second one, e.g., by exaggerating the aspiration of the first consonant in *hopper*, she seemed to have some aspiration left over for the next consonant. (The *p* was enunciated with an audible 'pop.') Without this extra aspiration on the first consonant, she seemed unable to articulate the second consonant. This might be thought of as a reduplication strategy that involves a phonological feature only. This appeared to be the same technique she was using during the short time she called Fred /had/. Until this time, as discussed earlier, she had called Fred *boy*, and justified it in her own way: the investigator said, "Can you say Fred?"

/no hi ə br/   'No, him a boy.'

The investigator asked, "A bur?"

/no, ə bO^i/   'No, a boy.'   The diphthong was not quite
    completed, however.   (2;4)

By the end of 2;11, after many practice sessions, she said /fwed/ with regularity.

An example of her drilling on *box* follows. In pretending to read a story from one of her books she said /bog^h/. The investigator asked "Hmm?" and she repeated very softly /bUkth/. The investigator asked "Box?" and she repeated again

/bok^h. . .bok^h. . .boksh/   'box'   (2;11)

The repetitions became louder as she became more confident. About ten minutes later, during this same 'story reading' session, she came to *box* again. This time she said /bawks/, articulating the consonants perfectly, but the vowel was too far back. She corrected herself twice, /boksh. . .boksh/, placing the vowel in the proper central position but losing the correct final consonant.

In the following example she was using an inadequate form while concentrating on a new meaning, when it occurred to her that she was not saying the word correctly: while she was eating lunch she broke her slice of cheese into two pieces and said

/E por a E por/   'This is one part and this is one part.'   (2;10)

As she said it she touched first one piece and then the other. As she ate the first half of the slice of cheese, she tore the other piece into 'parts' and went through the routine again and again until she had only tiny bits of cheese to work with. Then she did it with graham crackers, then with a quarter of an apple, pointing to the piece she had bitten off and was chewing on as /E por/

and what was left on the table as /E por/. Her last item of food was a box
of raisins, and she was trying to cut a raisin in two pieces with her front teeth
at which time she was discouraged from continuing the game. At one point
it occurred to her that she was saying /por/ instead of /port/ (part) and she
very deliberately articulared /p^{h}ort/ with a strong aspiration on the initial
consonant and also added the final consonant.

As time went on, Leslie continued to display her awareness of her inac-
curate reproductions of words, but she rarely rehearsed words openly later in
the way she did through her third year. However, she frequently corrected
her own pronunication, sometimes when someone didn't understand her, and
sometimes with no provocation. For example, in September she said

> We don't have /krisə/ lights, we don't. You do? (3;7)

The investigator didn't understand, and asked, "Don't have what?"

> I mean you got /krismə/ lights? 'Christmas tree lights'

She saw some out-of-season Christmas tree lights on a building across the street
and was unexpectedly discussing them. This is a word that might have been
recognized at Christmas time or if it had been within the framework of a previous conversation.

Other examples of her corrections follow. She was talking and drawing at
the same time, and said,

> I like this is /a poməs. . .hipoməs/ 'hippopotamus' (4;1)

> How come he has /theO. .thOz/ 'those' (4;7)

Evidence that she may have been rehearsing words privately at later ages
come from two kinds of incidents. First, there are cases such as the one mentioned in Chapter 5 in which she turned her head to the side so her mother
wouldn't see her practicing, while she rehearsed the word *vanilla*, and then
proudly used the word. Other instances involved her simply announcing that
as of that time she could say a certain word. For example,

> /don't say /aminO/ anymore. I say *animal*. (5;3)

After the middle of her fifth year, Leslie demonstrated the most difficulty
with words of more than two syllables and with medial consonant clusters.
She appeared to be working on the following words:

> /sudəntlE/ 'suddenly' (4;7)

/efənənt/   'elephant'   (4;7)

/skramlO/   'scrambled'   (4;7)

Suddenly was comparatively new in her active lexicon at this time and she was using it frequently, each time with a slightly different pronunciation. *Elephant* is one of the words she proudly announced following her fifth birthday that she could say correctly. There was a slight hesitation following the /m/ in *scrambled*, leading one to think she was concentrating on the pronunciation of the second syllable.

Bell suggests that the basis for the universality of the syllable is phonetic, and probably ultimately physiological.[8] Therefore, we conclude that a child such as Leslie, who has difficulty in early stages of speech production, will rely more heavily on the simplest form, the syllable, which is perceived as a whole, not a sequence of individual sounds.

General Phonological Development at
Later Ages

Whereas Leslie had been extremely difficult to understand at early stages in her speech development, by 4;9, when the Templin-Darley Articulation Test was given to her, she scored 48 correct out of 50 on the screening test where the mean score for girls her age was 40.6 (see Chapter 3 for discussion). Her performance on a word-by-word pronunciation test is better than her performance on similar items in conversation, but this is generally true, and whether there is more difference in her case than in any other child's is not known.

Early in her fifth year it could be said that, with the possible exception of occasional words, Leslie could be understood by most strangers. This represents rapid improvement in phonological development.

Discussion

In my review of the pertinent literature, I have not found any references, as reported in diaries and studies on child language acquisition, to children who appear to use either reduplication or consonant harmony to the extent that Leslie does. It is another example of her using a strategy that is not unique, but using it more extensively than other children appear to.

Likewise, no children have been found who seem to drill themselves on phonological problems in the way that Leslie does. It seems reasonable to assume that this self-tuition played an important role in enabling her to largely overcome her difficulties in this area. It is conceivable, but unlikely, that she would have made the dramatic progress she did without having been so diligent.

Notes

1. Roman Jakobson, *Child language aphasia and phonological universals* (The Hague: Mouton, 1968).
2. Ibid., p. 26.
3. M.M. Lewis, *Infant speech, A study of the beginnings of language* (New York: Humanities Press, 1951), pp. 31-32.
4. Ibid., p. 178.
5. E.C. Fudge, "Syllables," *Journal of Linguistics,* 1969, 5:253-86.
6. Werner F. Leopold, *Speech development of a bilinguial child,* Vol. 1. (Evanston, Ill.: Northwestern University Press, 1939), p. 5.
7. Nelson V. Smith, *The acquisition of phonology* (Cambridge, England: Cambridge University Press, 1973).
8. Alan E. Bell, "A state-process approach to syllabicity and syllable structure," Ph.D. dissertation, Stanford University, 1970.

5 Lexical Development and Multi-Purpose Words

Leslie had a large passive, or hearing, vocabulary, as indicated in Chapter 3 by her performance on the Peabody Picture Vocabulary Test, on which she ranked in the 99th percentile of children her age. Her active vocabulary has not been measured in any systematic way. In listening to her play with her three best friends in her neighborhood at 5;2, one got the distinct impression that her vocabulary was decidedly larger than that of the one child who was her own age, and was somewhat better than those of the two girls who were two years older than she. It was not comparable to Fred's active vocabulary at that age, however.

It has been claimed that while syntactic development proceeds at is own pace without the conscious knowledge of the child of its development and without being susceptible to instruction, the lexicon can be taught. (See Ervin-Tripp[1] and Cazden[2] for discussion and review.) Items may be added to a child's lexicon without his conscious knowledge, just as syntactical rules are, but lexical items may also be consciously added by the child.

An example of Leslie consciously adding a word to her lexicon follows. At 5;3 Leslie went out to the street with Fred to buy ice cream bars from the ice cream man. When they came in their mother asked what they got. Fred explained that he had Neopolitan, but Leslie seemed puzzled about what hers was even though she was eating it. Her mother looked at it and said, "Oh, you got vanilla." Leslie turned her head to the side so she was no longer facing her mother and muttered to herself for a minute or so. Then, turning her face toward her mother again, said, "Mom, listen to me. I got a vanilla bar." She had been furtively rehearsing the word *vanilla,* and as soon as she was confident she could say it to her own satisfaction, she said it.

One of the indications that she had difficulty in learning lexical items was that she frequently used morphological rules for arriving at lexical items rather than recalling words she had heard. Examples of this are: describing a picture of a woman sweeping, she said she was *brooming* (5;2); going barefoot was going *barefeeting* (4;5 to 5;3); and she referred to their clothes drier as a *drying machine* (4;11). She had heard the adult forms of all of these words at times, but not with great frequency. We have no way of knowing whether she did, in fact, formulate her own words according to morphological rules more often than most other children.

She also substituted phonetically similar words in many instances. For example, in referring to a felt-tip pen, she pointed to the lid and the "button," meaning the bottom half of the pen. All children appear to do this, and again, it can not be known whether Leslie engaged in it more often than most other children or not.

Multi-Purpose Words

Beginning at a very early point in her speech development, Leslie developed a strategy to alleviate her problem of a lack of as many lexical items as she needed in order to say what she wanted to say. She used a small group of substitute words which we are calling *multi-purpose* words. They appeared to substitute for lexical items she didn't know, couldn't recall, had not been able to analyze phonetically, or was unable to produce.

Slobin points out that people apparently find it easier to learn and store a smaller number of words, each with many senses, than to learn and store a separate phonetic form for each sense.[3] For example, the word-form *take* has 69 meanings listed in the dictionary. Slobin says "the more frequently a word is used, the more meanings it seems to have." Perhaps Leslie's strategy in using multi-purpose words is an extreme case of this kind of economy.

Adults as well as children sometimes use a substitute word or an indefinite word for one that is not known or cannot be recalled. According to Robertson and Cassidy, "We have a whole set of words, used conversationally when we either do not know, or cannot remember, or perhaps will not take the trouble to search for a more precise term: the *what-you-may-call-it* kind of word— *thingumabob, doohickie, jigger,* and so on."[4] Robertson and Cassidy refer to this as a process of generalization. Pound collected more than 100 such terms which she calls "indefinite names."[5]

Word Classes

Ervin-Tripp and Miller itemize some of the markers children may be thought to use in the process of learning to identify word classes: word order, suffixes such as *-ed, -s*, the use of articles to identify nouns, and prosody, or characteristic intonation and stress patterns, among others. They go on to explain that "morpheme classes can be divided into two groups, lexical and function classes. Lexical classes are few in number but have many members. In English these include nouns, verbs, adjectives, and certain adverbs. Function classes constitute a larger number of small, closed classes. In English these include conjunctions, prepositions, auxiliaries, and suffixes such as the plural and past tense morphemes."[6]

Bowerman also discusses this distinction between "functors" and "content" words, commenting on the absence of functors, or function words, at early stages of linguistic development.[7] Her Table 2 (p. 23) indicates that Seppo, the Finnish boy whose speech development she studied, used 8 functors at age 2;2 where 98 were required, and that Eve (from the Brown et al. study[8]) used 14 functors at 1;7 where 91 were required. Data from later ages are not available in her study.

In studying Leslie's use of her multi-purpose words, it is easy to assume that her lexicon fell into these two classes: functors and lexical, or content words. For a period of about two years (1;7 to 3;7) Leslie had two multi-purpose words, /E/~/A/ and /gEkIn/, which she used extensively. /E/~/A/ substituted in sentence positions where an adult would use a functor and /gEkIn/ (we will refer to this as *gi kine*) substituted for content words. No instances have been noted in which she used *gi kine* for a functor, nor does /E/~/A/ appear to substitute for a content word, though, as will be seen, the evidence is less clear-cut in the latter instance.

It might be noted here that Velten reported a swift development just beyond this time in his daughter Joan's use of prepositions, demonstratives, auxiliaries, articles, conjunctions, and the possessive and personal pronouns (between 2;3 and 2;6).[9] This was the same age at which Leslie greatly increased her use of her multi-purpose functors.

Another word Leslie used to some degree, but not as extensively as those just mentioned, was *do*. She used it as a multi-purpose verb, e.g.,

> Gwamma Gwampa do this a me. (2;1) She was showing a visitor the dress she was wearing. It had been given to her by her grandparents.

> Mommy, do mine. (2;2) She was asking her mother to put clothes on her doll.

> That is not good. That yukky. (The investigator asked, "Why's that yukky?" referring to a pen.)

> Cause I didn't want to do why. . .xxx getting my letter. (3;7)

At 4;1 her cousin Gregory asked "Can I do the organ?" meaning 'Can I play the organ?'

We have not attempted a study of the use of *do* by young children, but this does not appear to be an uncommon overgeneralization. *Do* is used in adult grammar to substitute for a verb in order to avoid repeating the verb twice, e.g., "I'll ask for you, as I always *do*." It may be this privilege of using *do* as a substitute verb that Leslie and Gregory, as well as many other children, have noted. Leslie used *do* correctly in the following case to substitute for a verb she had omitted in her first sentence:

> We don't one vase. Yes we do. (3;7) *Do* substitutes for *have*, which did not actually appear in the first sentence.

At this same age Leslie appears to have unnecessarily picked up the *do* from the investigator's question:

> I need different colors. (The investigator asked, "You do?
> What colors do you need?")

> Yellow and red or pink. Do need that. (3;7)

She had been using *do* for purposes of emphasis since about her second birthday, but judging from the lack of stress, this was not interpreted as the emphatic *do*.

Multi-Purpose Functor

Leslie's functors differed from Miller and Ervin-Tripp's operators[10] and Braine's pivots[11] in that they were not restricted to position in a two-word construction. They were active in her language development at a time when she was using utterances that were several morphemes long.

Leslie's multi-purpose functor was most often a front vowel, either /E/ or /A/, though sometimes she used /ə/ or /o/. It was not clear whether these represented separate entities to her or not, but we were unable to find a pattern in their variation. It was first thought the choice of /E/ or /A/, which occurred most prominently between 2;9 and 3;0, might be on the basis of vowel harmony:

> /A vA hr/ 'You stay here.' (2;9)

> /E wE mI/ 'will you read my book?" (2;10)

On close examination, however, this proved not to be consistent. The data was also examined to see if, in fact, /E/ substituted for some words and /A/ for others, but this failed also.

At 1;7 Leslie seemed to be using all four variants (/ə/, /o/, /E/, /A/) with equal frequency, but by 2;11 she was using either /E/ or /A/ most of the time. At this age (2;10 to 3;0) samples of her speech indicated that she was using this multi-purpose word to substitute for the following functors in the adult language: *the, these, a, and a, there's, where, in, on, to, it, it's, he, she, she's, his, I, I'll, you, your, my, is, was, and, after, will,* and *has.* Evidence that she was using the /E/~/A/ to substitute for these words came in part by her spontaneous utterances and in part from asking her to repeat short sentences (discussed below).

Many times it could not be determined what the /E/~/A/ substituted for, if anything, as in the following sentence. She was looking at a picture book and telling the story:

> /any E dir E nau E ka wE....E bOi E gU gub E bU bog^h/
> ' dinner now can   boy   box' (2;11)

The meaning of the above sentence is not known, and only the words that are glossed can be identified with any certainty. The listener could not be sure as to what, if anything, the /E/'s meant. Leslie, however, always gave the impression of fluency and of knowing what she was saying.

A listener might guess that Leslie is inserting this /E/~/A/ as a kind of place-holder in a sentence, functioning to maintain the intonation pattern. Since she didn't have a 'word' to use, she used a pro-word. This /E/~/A/ does not seem to function in the way the /m/ does, as reported by Engel[12] and Jespersen,[13] both of whom report its use as the child's sign that he wants something. Engel reports that the /m/ acts as an intonation carrier and that together (the /m/ and the intonation) are a means of expression before the child acquires 'words.' This humming (Summlaute) occurs at perhaps 7-10 months, an earlier age than that at which Leslie used the /E/~/A/.

Leslie's multi-purpose vowel does, however, resemble the /E/~/A/ that Bloom discusses in Eric's speech at Time III (1;10).[14] Bloom reports "Although the phonological element was /ə/ most often, there were variants, as in the examples with 'fit' (/ə fit, E fit/) and with nouns: '/E/ lamb' '/A/ bunny,' /E/ man,' '/E/ toy,' '/A/ baby,' and four occurrences of '/A/ naughty,' referring to a picture of naughty babies." Eric had *I* as a productive first person pronoun at this time, but he still appeared to use these other variants for *I*. Sometimes he seemed to use them for *it* and for *they*.

Guillaume reports that a French child, P, used a vowel sound, /o/, in much the same way: *A pu* (il n'y en a plus = there isn't any more), and *A peur* (j'ai peur = I'm frightened): age is not given for these utterances.[15] The same child at 1;3 said *A peur A peur A pu Bobo* (je l'ai mordue elle pleure, elle a mal, Jeannete = I bit her, she's crying, it's sore, Jeannette).

The same phenomenon appears to be taking place with the three children, Leslie, Eric, and P: the child is substituting a vowel sound for a variety of functors. From the data available, it appears that Leslie and P use this phonological element to replace more adult words than Eric does, with Leslie using it the most. It also appears that Leslie is using the substitute at a later chronological age as well as continuing it into a more advanced stage of language development than either of the other two children (see table 5-1), although we do not have information available regarding this aspect of Eric's and P's development as late at 3;7, so there is no conclusive evidence on this.

During an hour and twenty minutes of recorded conversation with Leslie early in 2;10, she used /E/~/A/ 134 times. During an equivalent time toward the end of 2;11 she used it 49 times. By this time she was beginning to replace it with better approximations of the various model functors.

By 1;11 she was using the first person possessive pronoun, *my*, occasionally, as in

My daddy! (1;11)

Table 5-1

Use of Multi-Purpose Functors (/E,A,o,ə/) by Three Children

Child	Age at Which Child Used Them
Leslie	1;7–3;7
Eric[a]	1;7–1;10
P[b]	1;2–1;5

---

[a]Data for Eric are from Lois Bloom, *Language Development: Form and Function in Emerging Grammars* (Cambridge, Mass.: M.I.T. Press, 1970).

[b]Data for P are from Paul Guillaume, "First stages of sentence formation in children's speech," *Studies in Child Language Development,* edited by Charles A. Ferguson and Dan I. Slobin (New York: Holt, Rinehart and Winston, 1973).

and also to mean *mine*, as when someone tried to take something away from her. By 2;2 she was noted using the adult form of *mine.* She was first noticed using the first person pronoun *I* at 2;4:

> /I ə wA wr/ 'I go that way, too.' She was pretending to
> shine her shoes, watching Fred shine his. (2;4)

Nevertheless, she used her multi-purpose vowel to substitute for these pronouns into her fourth year.

> /E tok E kI/ 'I talk this kind.' = 'I'm talking on the
> tape recorder.' (2;10)

She always used the adult form in an emphatic position. By the end of 2;11 she was using *I* more than 50 percent of the time where it was required.
Examples of her use of the multi-purpose functor follows:

> /ə gEgE/ 'a baby' (1;7)

> /*tha* ə gogE/ 'That's a doggie.' (1;11)

> /E ə nI br/ 'I have nice shoes,' or 'These are nice shoes.'
> (2;2)

> /E ku E nE/ 'She cut her knee.' (2;7)

> /E darzh/ 'These are stars.' (2;10)

/A kar A gOing/   'The car is going.'   (2;11)

/ə man E OnE wun br/   'A man gave us only one balloon.'   (2;10)

/E/   mommy bear go?   'Where did the mommy bear go?'   (2;10)

/E/   take my /gogE/   'Did you take my doggie?'   (3;3)

/E tAk E/ shoes off for?   'What did you take your shoes off for?   (3;3)

/E ə/   sit back watch me.   'You (just?) sit back and watch me.'   (3;2)

In the seventh example above, it appears that Leslie used her multi-purpose functor for the verb *gave*. How she viewed it cannot be known, of course. It might be hypothesized that her /E/~/A/ could substitute for verbs which did not seem to have a quality of action, whereas action verbs required *gi kine*, as will be seen below. *Gave* was not known to be in her active lexicon at this time. The most likely explanation for this sentence, however, is that she omitted the verb entirely, as she often did. The sentence would then read 'A man, he only one balloon.' She often used this non-standard construction, though it was not used by her family.

It might have been expected that she would insert her multi-purpose functor in the last sentence above to represent *and* between *back* and *watch* if she were using it as a place-holder. We have not measured pause lengths, however, to see if in some instances a pause may serve the same purpose.

Many of Leslie's utterances at this age and for several months to come could not be interpreted, and many of them were essentially just strings of vowel sounds to the listener.

Many instances of the use of this multi-purpose vowel seemed not to be substituting for a single word she didn't know, but to be substituting for more than one word or an entire construction of adult speech:

/E han wA/   'Move your hand away.'   (2;10)

/E mE/   'Is the phone call for me?'   (toy phone)   (2;10)

The examples given thus far have all been from spontaneous speech. At the end of Leslie's third year a list of the functors she was thought to be substituting /E/~/A/ for was compiled and incorporated into a list of twenty-five sentences for her to repeat. They were all given to her at 2;11, twelve one week and thirteen the next. Some were short, simple sentences, others were compound

sentences or were made complex in other ways. The principal objective in all
sentences was to see which elements of the model sentence would be replaced
by her multi-purpose functor. Some are modeled after Slobin and Welsh.[16]

The twenty-five sentences follow, first the model sentences given her to
repeat, then a transcription of her repetition of it, and a gloss of her transcription, where necessary. Notes are added in some instances.

Model: My house is brown.

/A mI haush i braun/

'Uh, my house is brown.'

This, and several other instances, suggest that Leslie may have used the /E/~/A/
sometimes in much the same way adults use *uh*.

Model: Today is Thursday.

/EdA E thrdA/

It may be noted that her word for *two* when she counts at this age is /tr/. The
fact that the *to* of *today* is unstressed may account for her substitution of /E/
here. The two forms may not bear any resemblance to each other, for her.

Model: The puppet bit the dog on TV.

/A gupə E   bit E   tEvE/

'The puppet bit   TV.'

The insertion of /E/ between *puppet* and *bit* might be interpreted as "the puppet,
he" or perhaps another *uh* while she tried to remember the remainder of the sentence. She was having difficulty, as may be seen from her omission of *dog*. It
appears here, and in many of the following sentences that were more complex
than she usually produced, that she was not processing the sentence for meaning
and restructuring it, but was trying to remember its acoustic quality and reproduce it.

Model: Jerry who cried came to my house.

/A eE   kwI   ə   mI hauth/

'Uh, Jerry cried   my house.'

This sentence was modeled after Slobin and Welsh's sentence "Mozart who cried came to my party."[17] Echo's imitation was "Mozart came to my party," omitting entirely the embedded clause. Echo was 2;3. Leslie, on the other hand, included the *cried* from the embedded clause, but /ə/ cannot be assumed to be the verb of the main clause, or any other specific word. At this time, *come* was in her lexicon, but *came* was not.

Model: The cookie the cookie monster ate was chocolate.

/E   kUkE   gogr   E   gUkE*th*/

'The cookie monster eats cookies.'

Model: Here is a brown brush and here is a comb.

/ə   i   bush   e   i   kOm/

'Here is brush   here is comb.'

The /e/ and /i/ here seem more to represent her best approximation of the words being modeled, rather than being variants of her multi-purpose functor. On this same sentence, Echo repeated "Here's a brown brush an' a comb," (2;3) maintaining all the essential elements, but deleting the second clause, whereas Leslie maintained both clauses, but deleted the adjective.

Model: My shoes are here and the tree is green.

/A   mI   shUzh   E   O. . . . .   gEn/

'Uh, my shoes are,   ohhh. . . . green.'

The fact that the two clauses of this "sentence" are completely unrelated makes it something of a non-sentence, and greatly increases its difficulty for imitation. Leslie's "Ohhh" was due to her total dismay at being unable to remember the remainder of the sentence. With a similar sentence, "The batman got burned and the big shoe is here," Echo said, "Big shoe is here and a big shoe is here." She acknowledged the presence of two clauses by repeating the same one twice.

Model: The candles are burning on the table.

/A   ka   A A A   em   A   kAO   E   br   E bir tEO/

'The can. . .   candle is burn. .is burning   table.'

Some of the /A/'s here represent Leslie's preparation to try to correct her pronunciation of *candle* from /ka/ to /kaO/. The /E bir/ represents a clarification of *burning*, along with, presumably, her substitution of the auxiliary verb. /bir/ would not seem to be an improvement over /br/ unless one assumes that this second attempt is including, for her, some element of *ing*.

Model: My mommy plays songs for me on the piano.

/E mI momE E fA pa *thə* m   mE/

'Uh, my mommy plays piano for   m– me.'

The /E/ following *mommy* may represent the construction, "Mommy, she plays," or it may be more in the nature of *uh* as she tries to recall the remainder of the sentence. There seems to be a clarification of *me*.

Model: It's warm inside and it's cold outside.

IE   wOi   EthId   E   kUth EthId/

'It's warm inside it's cold inside.'

While *inside* is a word she used quite often, *outside* was not known to be in her active lexicon. At a later age, when she wanted to go outside (to the back yard) she used her own morphological rules for formulate *backside*. The use of *inside* for both *inside* and *outside* may also represent the positive member of a pair of lexical items which is learned first and overgeneralized to include both members of the pair. As with polar adjectives, discussed below, both members of the pair share semantic features.

Model: The boy was happy to go to the party.

/A bOi   E thad   ev   hOi/

'The boy was sad   party.' Or 'The boy he was sad.'

Since /ev/ does not have apparent phonetic similarity to the words that were omitted from the model, *to go to the*, it can't be known what this represented to Leslie. /E/~/A/ was used earlier in the sentence as would be predicted. Her substitution of *sad* for its polar adjective, *happy*, follows the prediction of Olson that if a contrastive adjective is not remembered exactly, or a close synnonym used, its polar adjective is most likely to be substituted (as in this case) because it contains all but one of the same semantic features.[18,19] The nature of the adjectival predication will be remembered even if the exact value of the predication is not. Olson's hypothesis was borne out in the analysis of the adjectives used in a story-retelling project involving Yakima Indian and non-Indian children, also.[20]

Model: The man who was on TV was Misterogers.

/A   man   E   tE   E   washəsh/

'   man   TV   Misterogers.'

At this time, *who* was not in Leslie's active lexicon, nor did it appear to be one of the functors for which /E/~/A/ could substitute. At this time she had not started asking *who* questions, and *who* clauses appeared to be beyond her productive competence.

Model: I will do it for Grandpa.

/A   A   dU   i   bopo/

'I (will?) do   it   Grandpa.'

Model: His nose is big and a tiny bit red.

/hE no*th* E bEg a   wA wA   wed/

'His nose is big and way, way   red.'

It is not certain, but most likely, that the /wA wA/ here is Leslie's *way, way*, a variation of *away*, with the general meaning of "to a considerable degree." She used this term upon occasion. If this is correct, she is again assigning the polar meaning to the adjectives *tiny bit*.

Model: Will you come to my house?

/A   kum   mI hauth/

'   come   my house?'

This is another example of uncertainty as to what the initial /A/ represents from Leslie's point of view. Perhaps she simply recognized that there was something at the beginning of the sentence and this fills that slot. Since Leslie regularly omitted auxiliaries, /A/ more likely represents *you* than *will*, but it may represent both.

Model: There's a yellow schoolbus going down the street.

/A *the*O   dI   kUbuth   E   dwEp/

'Uh, there's yellow schoolbus   street.'

There is one of the functors Leslie had been thought to be using /E/~/A/ for, and this attempt at a replication is the first recorded for her.

Model: I will watch your baby while he plays.

/I   wosh   U   bAbE   E   fwAd/

'I   watch your baby   he   plays'   (or possibly, 'he's afraid.')

While it is represented here as though /E/ substitutes for *he*, it is just as likely that it represents *while he*. There is no evidence that the /E/~/A/ substitutes only for words that are phonetically similar to the multi-purpose functor.

Model: I'll do it in a minute.

/I   DU   i   mitit/

'I   do it   minute.'

Model: I don't want to do it.

/I   ewE   dU   it/

'I   do   it.'

/ewE/ cannot be glossed with any certainty. Leslie shook her head while she was saying this sentence, and this (the head shake), perhaps plus /ewE/, may be thought of as the negative element in the sentence.

Model: I will be three years old pretty soon.

/I   thE   Oi   iE   U/

'I   three old pretty soon.'

This sentence offers an example of Leslie's reliance on vowels, mentioned above.

Model: Your foot is inside of your shoe and sock.

/A   fEt   EsId   thU thokth thUtsh/

'Your feet inside   shoe   sox   shoes.'

The last word appeared to be an attempt to make *shoe* plural. Leslie may have thought something was missing, and that the plural was what it was. The fact that she made *foot* plural reinforces this assumption. This is an instance of her early use of *feet* for plural. A little later, she began to use the form *foots*, continuing it through 5;2.

Model: The doll has a red purse and a red hat.

/A do A   pUrsh A do A en hat/

'   doll   purse   doll   red hat.'

Model: A mommy and a baby sat in a chair.

/A momE A bAbE sat E krer/

' mommy   baby   sat   chair.'

Model: There's no more.

/A   nO mOr/

'   no more.'

Model: My mommy made a Beezie for Jason.

/ mI momE mAk E vE*th* E vE*th*inth/

'Uh, my mommy make a Beezie   Jason.'

Beezie was a toy clown and Jason was a friend of Leslie's.

It will be seen that there is not a one-to-one relationship between functors in the model sentences and Leslie's multi-purpose functor. In this and other respects, her performance in spontaneous and imitated utterances is not very different.

From about 3;3 on, Leslie used noticeably fewer of these multi-purpose vowels. By the middle of her fourth year few words were omitted, with the exception of a number of common verb forms and articles:

> Fred not /gr/ 'Fred's not a girl.' (3;6)

> We don't one vase. 'We don't have a vase.' Or, 'We don't
> have a vase like that one.' (3;7)

Upon examination, it can be seen that many of the elements she had been omitting were items she was capable of producing phonetically.

Multi-Purpose Content Words

Leslie's most frequently used multi-purpose content word was /gEkIn/, derived from *this kind*. This word could substitute for a noun, verb, adjective, or a demonstrative pronoun.

Gi kine was used by Leslie much as speakers of Hawaiian creole (called pidgin English by its speakers) use 'da kine,' derived from *that kind*, according to Linda T. Tani,[a] a native speaker. She reports that *da kine* is used whenever one cannot think of a word (usually a noun or adjective) that expresses their intentions more precisely. Examples offered by Miss Tani are "Da kine person, he real nice," or "You know da kine." The meaning is usually made clear by the context, by facial expressions, and gestures. Pidgins, and creoles in early stages, such as the Hawaiian creole, typically have small vocabularies, which accounts for the extensive use of multi-purpose expressions such as *da kine*. The same reason, that is, a small active vocabulary, appears to account for Leslie's use of *gi kine*. Ferguson has pointed out that pidgins and a child's early speech are simplified in some of the same ways.[21] This is one example.

Examples of Leslie's use of *gi kine* follow.

Substituting for nouns:

> /E gEkIn on/   'Is the tape recorder on?' (2;10)

> /gEkIn gwEn/ 'The cuff is green.' Pointing to the cuff of
> her sleeve. (2;11)

---

[a]Used by permission, from a term paper prepared by Linda T. Tani for the author's class in Language in Culture and Society, Spring, 1974.

Substituting for verbs:

When asked what the owl in a picture was doing she said:

> /E gEkI/ 'He does this.'   Then she made a pounding noise
> with her fist. The owl was pounding with a hammer.   (2;10)

Substituting for demonstrative pronoun:

> /gEkIn do E fiming do/ 'This doll is a swimming doll.'
> She bent the arms and legs of the doll back and showed how
> the doll swam.   (2;11)

> Gi kine guy green eyes. 'This teddy bear has green eyes.'

Asked what she was drawing, she answered:

> /EkIn/ a duck. Mad duck.   'This kind of a duck.   A mad
> duck.'   (3;7)

By this time, the initial *g* was nearly always dropped.

Leslie did not use /gE/ by itself to mean *this*. By 2;11 she had begun to use /thi/ or /thith/ for *this*. As she approached 3;0 she was using /thith/ perhaps 50 percent of the time for *this*, but never as a substitute for the first segment of *gi kine*. She does not seem to equate the *gi* of *gi kine* with *this*, but she does seem to equate *kine* with *kind*. She improved her articulation of the second element of *gi kine* using *kind* as the model. At first it was /kI/, then /kIn/ and as she approached 3;0, she occasionally added the final consonant.

She also preceded /kI/ with /u/ to mean *other kind*. While listening to her grandfather play the piano, she said,

> /momE pA paO u kI/ 'Mommy plays the piano another way.'
> (2;10)

During a sample of an hour and twenty minutes of recording of conversation with Leslie during the early part of 2;10, she used *gi kine* 14 times. During a similar sample taken at the end of 2;11 she used it 18 times. The difference is undoubtedly due to change. It appears that her use of *gi kine* neither diminished nor increased during this two-month period, but toward the end of 2;11 she occasionally used *thing* or *something* where she might once have used *gi kine*.

Thing is one of the general terms in the adult lexicon, and there is no way of determining whether or not Leslie might have used this, as well as *something*, more often than other children, but we would speculate that she did during her fourth and fifth years. The following conversation typifies her attitude:

/i *th*ith kod/ 'What is this called?'

Then, answering her own question, she said,

/fing/ 'Thing.'

The investigator said, "I thought it was called a knife." Leslie answered,

/i/ not a knife.   It picks fings up.   Toys up.   (3;4)

Although the word *toys* has been in her active lexicon for some time at 3;0, Leslie explained as she went to her room to bring out more toys:

I more /thing*th*/   'I'll get more things (toys).'

Another indefinite word she used, though only for animate nouns, or objects to which she attributed animacy, was *guys*, or *guy*. She used this to refer to people whether their names were known or not. When her mother and brother walked in the door she turned to the investigator and said,

/gIth/ 'Guys!' (Mommy and Fred have arrived!)

Or at the airport, looking at the crowds of people, she said,

/*th*E gIth/ 'See all the people.'

At 5;2 she still used *guys* excessively.

We note that the child, P, studied by Guillaume, also had a general purpose word.[22] At 1;2 P used *ato*, derived from "marteau," which means *hammer*, for the following items: buttonhook, hand mirror, comb, handbag, a casserole, hairpin, wooden spade, key, gun, box, belt, wallet, ruler, puttees, bowl, safety pin, night light, coffee grinder, plate, and spoon. Guillaume points out (p. 536) that this "master word" never refers to people, animals, or food: it is equivalent to *machin* (gadget) or *chose* (thing).

As might be guessed from the more general nature of the term from which *gi kine* is derived (*this kind*), Leslie's word had wider applicability than P's. Her principal restriction on it seemed to be that it was not used for people.

Discussion

It is apparent that along with her difficulty in acquiring the phonological system of her language, Leslie also had more than the usual amount of difficulty in acquiring an active vocabulary. That is, her lexicon building did not keep pace with what one would expect of a child of her exceptional abilities in other areas. No simple explanation for this offers itself, but it would seem that the learning of functors and of content words may involve different processes. Functors are short, perhaps more easily articulated than many content words, if one knows them. On the other hand, they are usually unstressed, and so may not be easily available to the child for phonological analysis. In conversation as well as in storytelling (or pretending to read from a book), where her intonation patterns were somewhat exaggerated, Leslie's multi-purpose functors were always at low levels of her intonation patterns and unstressed.

It has been pointed out many times that language is redundant—the meaning can be retained even though some elements are omitted in speech. It is possible that Leslie comprehends language without the assistance of functors. It might even be thought that Leslie believes she is duplicating adult forms with her place-holders. Another, perhaps better, possibility is that she distinguishes the adult forms as being distinctive, just as Joan Velten, for example, obviously did, and she comprehends their meaning to approximately the same extent other children do, but she is less capable of analyzing the words acoustically for reasons which are not known.

The less common lexical items may often be learned as described by Hebb, Lambert, and Tucker by means of transient one-trial learning without reinforcement, as mentioned in Chapter 2.[23] It can be categorized as 'acquisition of information.' At earlier ages, with more frequently used lexical items, particularly nouns, active teaching sometimes takes place in the home. A mother may say to the child, "This is a cup. Can you say cup?" And if the child says *cup* or anything remotely resembling it, he is praised. Lexical items used less frequently and at later ages are not so apt to be treated this way.

The less frequently used content words are the ones we would expect Leslie to have some difficulty with since one-time auditory input does not appear to be an efficient mode of learning for her. This appears to be the case, judging from her extensive use of multi-purpose content words.

Notes

1. Susan M. Ervin-Tripp, "An overview of theories of grammatical development," in *The ontogenesis of grammar: A theoretical symposium,* edited by Dan I. Slobin (New York: Academic Press, 1971), pp. 189-212.
2. Courtney B. Cazden, *Child language and education* (New York: Holt, Rinehart and Winston, Inc., 1972).
3. Dan I. Slobin, *Psycholinguistics* (Glenview, Illinois: Scott, Foresman and Co., 1971).
4. Stuart Robertson, and Frederic G. Cassidy, *The development of modern English,* 2nd ed. (Englewood Cliffs, N.J.: Prentice-Hall, 1954), p. 237.

5. Louise Pound, "American indefinite names," *American Speech* 6 (1931): 257-59.
6. Susan M. Ervin-Tripp, and Wick R. Miller, "Language development," *Child psychology, 62nd yearbook, National Society for the Study of Education*, Part I, edited by H.W. Stevenson (Chicago: University of Chicago Press, 1963), pp. 108-143.
7. Melissa Bowerman, *Early syntactic development* (London: Cambridge University Press, 1973).
8. Roger Brown, Courtney Cazden and Ursula Bellugi-Klima, "The child's grammar from I to III," in *Minnesota Symposia on Child Psychology*, vol. II, edited by J.P. Hill (Minneapolis: University of Minnesota Press, 1968), pp. 28-73.
9. H.V. Velten, "The growth of phonemic and lexical patterns in infant language," *Language* 21 (1943):281-92.
10. Wick Miller, and Susan M. Ervin, "The development of grammar in child language," in *The acquisition of language,* edited by Ursula Bellugi and Roger Brown, Monographs of the Society for Research in Child Development, vol. 29, No. 1, 1964, pp. 9-34.
11. Martin D.S. Braine, "The ontogeny of English phrase structure: The first phase," in *Child Language: A book of readings,* edited by Aaron Bar-Adon and Werner F. Leopold (Englewood Cliffs, New Jersey: Prentice-Hall, 1971), pp. 279-89.
12. W. von Raffler Engel, "Die entwicklung vom laut zum phonem in der kindersprache," *Proceedings of the Fifth International Congress of Phonetic Sciences*, Muster, 1964, edited by E. Swirner and W. Bethge (Basel: Karger,1965), pp. 482-85.
13. Otto Jespersen, *Language, its nature, development and origin* (New York: W.W. Norton, 1922)
14. Lois Bloom, *Language development: Form and function in emerging grammars* (Cambridge, Mass.: M.I.T. Press, 1970), pp. 117-18.
15. Paul Guillaume, "First stages of sentence formation in children's speech," in *Studies in child language development,* edited by Charles A. Ferguson and Dan I. Slobin (New York: Holt, Rinehart and Winston, 1973), pp. 529-34.
16. Dan I. Slobin, and Charles A. Welsh, "Elicited imitation as a research tool in developmental psycholinguistics," *Studies in child language development,* edited by Charles A. Ferguson and Dan I. Slobin (New York: Holt, Rinehart and Winston, Inc., 1973), pp. 485-97.
17. Ibid., p. 487.
18. Gary M. Olson, "On the congnitive structure of noun phrases: memory for prenominal adjectives in ordinary English sentences," Ph.D. dissertation, Stanford University, 1970.
19. Gary M. Olson, "Memory for prenominal adjectives in ordinary English sentences," *Cognitive Psychology* 2 (1971):300-312.

20. Thelma E. Weeks, and John R. Weeks, "Some measures of the relation between linguistic and cognitive skills in young Yakima Indian and non-Indian children," unpublished paper, Stanford University, 1973.
21. Charles A. Ferguson, "Absence of copula and the notion of simplicity: A study of normal speech, baby talk, foreigner talk and pidgins," in *Social factors in pidginization and creolization*, edited by Dell Hymes (New York: Cambridge University Press. 1971).
22. Guillaume, "First stages of sentence formation in children's speech."
23. D.O. Hebb, W.E. Lambert, and G.R. Tucker, "Language, thought and experience," *Modern Language Journal* 54 (1971): 212–22.

6 Development of Imperatives

The imperative is defined (Webster's III) as the grammatical mood that expresses the will to influence the behavior of another as in a command, entreaty or exhortation. Lyons points out that

> Since commands or instructions are generally issued directly to the hearer, what one might call the "central" class of imperative sentences are associated with the "second person"; and it is a rather striking fact that in very many languages which inflect the verb for person, number, tense, mood, etc. (including the Indo-European languages) the form of the verb which occurs in "second person singular" imperative sentences is uninflected for all these categories (i.e. it is identical with the stem).[1]

In standard English, then, there is no way in which the verb of the imperative sentence is necessarily imperative in meaning: English has no imperative as separate morphological category. And for the very young child, the form of the imperative verb is identical to the verb form used for all sentences—the uninflected or unmarked verb form.

Since the imperative normally lacks a surface subject and the verb is uninflected, there is generally no structural marking of the child's imperative form; young children produce sentences with the same syntactic structure which are not imperatives, as mentioned above. Bowerman says that though both Seppo and Rina (Finnish children) produced many utterances designed to influence the actions of others, these were not usually formally marked as imperatives, although in Finnish verbs are inflected for the imperative, and neither child consistently omitted the subject.[2]

Bloom[3] and Brown, Cazden, and Bellugi-Klima[4] both mention the lack of imperative markers in the child's speech, although Brown et al. (p. 41) indicate that there were a few words the child learned to use after Stage I, especially *please* and *gimme*, which could be confidently interpreted as imperative markers.

Leslie quite consistently used the prosodic markers of loud voice and higher pitch than usual for imperatives until around her fourth birthday, at which point she began to use adult syntactic markers for other sentences, offering a contrast to the imperatives.

By the time Leslie was 1;5 she had at least five monoremes which she used upon occasion as imperatives (Halliday's regulatory function in Phase I of language acquisition[5]): /ʔu/, her word for *notice*, which she used as a command for someone to pick up something she had dropped from the high chair, to order someone to watch her do something, etc. For example, Leslie was accustomed to having Fred notice and comment on her new dresses or hair ribbons. At 1;5 she was wearing a new dress for the first time when Fred came in from play. She stood waiting for him to comment but he walked past without noticing her at all. She followed him until he stopped and she touched him on the stomach and said /ʔu/. He was busy and still didn't look at her. She waited a second and then hit him on the stomach and said /ʔu/ louder and pulled her skirt out in front of her. He finally looked at her and said, "Oh, you have on a new dress!" She laughed out loud and twisted around a little, her hands on her dress to show her appreciation for the nice compliment, even though she had had to ask for it.

Other monoremes, such as

/alalalala/   'water'   (1;5)   (where the /l/ is a flap)

/ʔulk/   'milk'   (1;5)

were both used as imperatives in requesting drinks. The same words with different intonation contours were used to say something like "The water has been spilled," or "Fred is drinking milk." /dada/ and /momo/ were both used as imperatives also, meaning "Come here!" "Pick me up" or simply "Smile at me!" She also used these monoremes in talking to other people, as though to announce to them, "That's my daddy," or something of that nature. These monoremes could also be used with a question intonation to ask "Where is Mommy?" While the total context of the situation was the most compelling indication of the imperative nature of the monoreme, paralinguistic features, such as volume and intonation served as the linquistic indicators.

These imperatives follow the usual monoreme type of imperatives found in the earliest speech development of young children. McNeill says "Holophrastic speech means that while children are limited to uttering single words at the beginning of language acquisition, they are capable of conceiving of something like full sentences."[6] For example, Hildegard at 1;8 used *mit* to mean "Come with," and *away* to mean "Put it away." It is not always possible, however, to pick such imperatives out of the diaries which have been kept of other children because the person keeping the diary must make note of when the word is used as an imperative. For example, Bloom reports that Eric at Stage II (1;8) said 'play it,' 'get it,' and 'show me,'[7] all of which have the usual syntactic pattern of the imperative, but only 'show me' was an imperative. The first two may fit into what Leopold calls a 'self-imperative,' however.[8]

"Watch-me!" Construction

At 2;6 Leslie started using the imperative,

/wosh mE/   'Watch me!' or 'Pay attention to me!'   (2;6)

This imperative was used many times a day when she wanted family members or the investigator to take note of such accomplishments as being able to jump off a small step, stand on one foot, or anything judged to be worth a few seconds of attention. It had been used perhaps a hundred times or more before the other "Watch-me!" constructions were noted.

By 2;10 she also used it to mean 'listen to me.' For example, while someone was reading to her about cows, she said "Watch me! Cow say 'moo moo'." Other times it seems to mean both 'watch' and 'listen': at 3;0 she was sitting inside a large cardboard carton with a hole torn in the side. She said, "Watch me!" and she put both hands through the hole and squeezed them together and moved her fingers in various ways while she said "woof, woof." The investigator said, "Oh, your *hands* are making the noise!"   She said, "No. Doggie say woof woof."

Bloom also reports that Eric at Stage III (1;10) used "watch noise!" for 'listen to the noise' when he was making a noise with the tinker toys.[9]

Starting at 2;8 and continuing through 3;0 Leslie used a large number of other imperatives on the same pattern as "Watch me":

/fefn mE/ 'Blanket me!' or 'Cover me with the blanket!'
     (/fefn/ originally referred to a sweater, then was generalized
     to include other fuzzy things, such as blankets and sleepers.)

Coat me!   'Put my coat on me!'

Dress me!   'Put my dress on me!'   It should be noted that the
     meaning of this adult-sounding imperative did not coincide
     precisely with the usual adult meaning. Leslie's meaning was
     limited to the gloss suggested whereas adult meaning would
     be "Put my clothes on me."

Paper me!   'Give me a piece of paper!'

Pencil me!   'Give me a pencil!'

Color book me!   'Give me a color book!'

Butter me!   'Butter my bread!"

Water me!   'Give me a drink of water!'

Apple me !   'Give me an apple!'

Pepper me!   'Put some pepper on my food!'

Slippers me!   'Put my slippers on me!'

Milk me!   'Give me a drink of milk!'

Up me!   'Pick me up!'   Gregory used this same construction
    with the same meaning at 1;5. Leslie's cousin Jennifer used
    just "Up!" with the same meaning at 0;9.

Down me!'   'Put me down!'

More me!   'Give me more!'   At least once, at 3;0, she used this
    to mean "Wash my hands again!"

This construction worked for Leslie. It was invariably understood by family
members, and she seldom had occasion to use it with strangers. For a child who
had trouble making herself understood, this may have been the determining factor
in her frequent use of the pattern.

Perhaps it should also be noted here that this construction is not an unusual
one in adult speech. "Watch me!", which it was apparently patterned after, is
standard. There are also other similar surface structures with underlying structures
that are different from that of *watch me*, such as "Butter me my blue," (Joan
Rubin, personal communication), translated as "Butter this blueberry muffin for
me." This corresponds precisely to the meaning of Leslie's 'butter me!' The
meaning of all of these fixed-pattern imperatives is invariably "Do something for
or to me." In the case of the gloss of 'butter me' it is the object, or patient (that
which is being acted upon), that is missing. However, it might be more accurate
to have glossed this imperative as "Put some butter on my bread," and 'blanket
me' as "Put the blanket on me." In this way, the translations would match the
others in regard to what is omitted: the usual adult verb (put, give, pick) and
the functor, and in adult speech these verbs as well as the functors would tend
to be unstressed in these imperatives.

Imperatives with an Expressed Subject

It is interesting to note that in baby talk and foreigner talk, the subject of an
imperative is more often included in the surface structure than in unmarked
speech.[10] Not only are subjects more often expressed in imperatives directed to a
child, but a child has a larger proportion of imperatives directed to him than an

adult normally does. In spite of this, in the first stage of language acquisition, a child's imperatives do not have an expressed subject. However, in the second stage, they frequently do. After this stage, the child normalizes the imperative again, and follows the more usual adult form.

Leslie followed this pattern, as did Hildegard. Leopold reports that while at 1;10 Hildegard used the form /dash mE/ "Dress me!' by 2;1 she used the following imperatives: "You scratch my back," "You button my shoe," and "You eat your pudding," and 2;4 "You tell me," and 2;6, speaking about a napkin, "I say /napənt/, you say in German, Mama."[11]

At 2;9 Leslie started using imperatives that went beyond the two-word formulation and included *you*:

> /A vA hr/ 'You stay here.' The /A/ is assumed to sub-
> stitute for *you* (see Chapter 5). (2;10)

> /A theE *thEth*/ 'You see these.' She gave the viewer to the
> investigator with this instruction to look at the pictures.
> (2;11)

> /U hOd *th*is ə mE/ 'You hold this for me.' (3;1)

> /Enink. . .Edink bak/ 'You lean back.' *You lean* was
> repeated in an apparent attempt to pronounce it correctly.
> (3;2).

> /E ə/sit back watch me. 'You (just?) sit back and watch
> me.' (3;2)
> /U/ come me. 'You come with me.' (3;3)

Later imperatives seldom included the subject.

The first imperatives that seemed to incorporate an auxiliary verb form were negative imperatives at 3;7:

> Don't go all alone in the office. (3;7)

> Don't do that. (3;7)

However, Bellugi, in discussing Adam, Eve, and Sarah's negations, points out that "We did not analyze *can't* and *don't* as part of the auxiliary verbs for the children, partly on the ground that auxiliary verbs were missing from declarative sentences and questions, and occurred with many restrictions with particular verbs only."[12] This was true of Leslie, also, and we may assume that *don't* was learned as a single lexical item.

Later Imperatives

Some examples of Leslie's imperatives beyond the 'Watch me' pattern imperatives follow:

My turn! This started at 2;4 and was used very frequently and for a variety of purposes, such as to get into a conversation—it was her turn to talk. This imperative was somewhat over-generalized in meaning—the reverse of 'dress me,' which was restricted in meaning. This included the adult meaning of 'my turn!', but also included non-adult meanings, such as "That's my toy" (no one else gets a turn with it!). These non-adult meanings dropped off and by about 4;0, she used this imperative with generally adult meanings.

/ver/! 'Come here!' (starting at 2;8)

/Ak E han der/! 'Take (put) your hand there.' That is, "Hold the page of the book open for me!" (2;10)

/kOth on/! 'Put my clothes on me!' (2;11)

Off my dress! 'Take my dress off me!' (3;0)

Off sox! 'Take my sox off!' (3;0)

Sit down! (3;0)

Close drapes! (3;0)

High them! 'Put them up high.' (3;0)

Off this! 'Turn this off.' (3;2)

Watch this! (3;4)

Come here! (3;4)

Now, stay like you were! (4;4)

Hold this right here! (4;4)

And the owl said "Get me outta here!" (4;7)

Discussion

In an attempt to explain Leslie's use of nouns, such as *apple* and *color book,* as verbs in her "Watch-me!" construction, we would like to suggest the possibility of non-distinction in the underlying forms for Leslie between nouns and verbs. Other examples of this same phenomenon may be occurring in declarative sentences without being recognized as such. For example, we translated Leslie's sentence:

> /O e bEbE gwA he wAi u hE bAbE bau/ 'Oh, when baby
> Greg he wakes up, he has a baby bottle.' (2;10)

However, maybe/hE bAbE bau/ is equivalent to *color book me* where the underlying categorization of the noun is concerned. We assume she has a copula in the underlying form, but there is no real evidence of this. Perhaps she means to be saying "He baby-bottles."

A number of linguists have adopted Austin's analysis of the imperative as being a 'performative.'[13] Austin specifies that a performative does something, e.g., "I name this ship the Queen Elizabeth" as uttered when smashing the bottle against the stem; and that the performative is 'happy or unhappy as opposed to true or false,' e.g., if the umpire says 'out' the batter is 'out' whether the umpire's verdict is justified or not.

Austin has isolated five classes of performatives: (1) verdictives, (2) exercitives, (3) commissives, (4) behavitives, and (5) expositives. Imperatives are one of the exercitives, which includes the exercising of powers, rights, or influence.

These five classes of verbs presumably include every English verb as a performative verb and therefore the underlying structure of the declarative sentence 'The man hit the ball' would be (Sentence 1) 'I say to you' + (Sentence 2) 'The man hit the ball,' and the imperative sentence 'You come here' would be (Sentence 1) 'I command you' + (Sentence 2) 'You come here.'

On the basis of this general analysis, Langendoen[14] suggests that the underlying structure for the sentence:

> Take these clothes to the laundry.

would be as shown in Figure 6-1.

Langendoen does not discuss at any length the import of the imperative marker, but the surface structure realization of this is a great deal more than just the syntactic structure. For Leslie, prosodic marking such as loud voice, higher pitch than usual in the surface structure is required in order to fulfill the underlying specification of 'imperative.' It is not known how generally true this is for other children.

Discussing the diagram, Langendoen says, "The abstract imperative

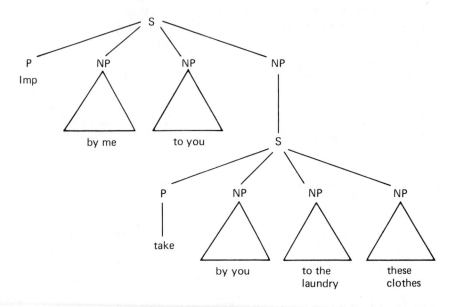

Figure 6-1.   Langendoen's (1969) Deep Structure of an Imperative Sentence.

Source: D. Terence Langendoen, *The Study of Syntax: The Generative-Trans-formational Approach to the Structure of American English.* Copyright © 1969 by Holt, Rinehart and Winston, Inc. Reprinted by permission of Holt, Rinehart and Winston, Inc.

Note: Symbols used in the figure are: P = Predicate; Imp = imperative marker; S = Sentence; NP = Noun Phrase; triangles stand for internal structure of the sentence that is irrelevant to the present discussion.

predicate is a three-place predicate, two of whose arguments[a] are fixed. The agent is expressed always by the first-person pronoun, and the dative by the second-person pronoun (or an NP co-referential with it). The third argument is the content of the command, and in it the second-person pronoun must occur as an agent."

Following this pattern, the imperative sentence used by Leslie at 2;9,

Apple me!   'Give me an apple.'

---

[a]Langendoen defines *argument of a predicate* as "A noun phrase which is a member of the same constituent as that predicate."[15]

would be:

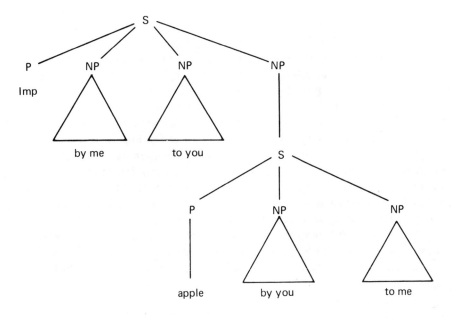

Figure 6-2. Underlying Structure of Leslie's Imperative "Apple me!", following Langendoen.[a]

[a]D. Terence Langendoen, *The Study of Syntax: The Generative-Transformational Approach to the Structure of American English* (New York: Holt, Rinehart and Winston, Inc., 1968.

Langendoen's definition of a predicate (p. 153) is "(1) The verb phrase of a sentence. (2) The deep-structure category which, together with arguments, constitutes sentences. Surface-structure nouns, verbs, and adjectives are all predicates."

In discussing relative clause transformation and the substitution of indefinite pronouns for the nouns (pp. 76-78) Langendoen suggests "Suppose further that it could be shown that every occurrence of every noun in every deep structure of every sentence of English is as a predicate noun to some indefinite pronoun (say *one*, or *thing*) as in Bach.[16] Then we could hold that the entire semantic representation of nouns is in terms of selectional features, too, just like those of verbs and adjectives. Nouns would only take on feature specifications upon substitution for one or the other of the indefinite pronouns. This would effectively mean that as far as deep structures are concerned, the categorial distinction between nouns, verbs, and adjectives is irrelevant. These would be surface-structure distinctions only. The position that every noun in English occurs as a predicate in deep structure receives empirical support from a variety of considerations."

While the problem being discussed by Langendoen was different than our problem with Leslie's predicates in her imperative sentences (his nouns and adjectives are combined with copulas), we would like to extend his proposal of non-distinction in the underlying structure of nouns, adjectives, and verbs as a possible means of accounting for the predicate of 'apple me' (fig. 6-2) being a noun. It seems that this non-distinction of categories, or state of neutrality (a continuation for Leslie, perhaps, of the ability of monoremes to function variously), in the underlying structure is evidenced also in English by adults through the use of metaphors or in casual speech, which is as innovative as the more artistic innovations of poets and creative writers. For example, *blanket* was a noun borrowed from Old French into Middle English. There had to be a first time that it was used as a verb, as in "The snow blankets the hillside." Likewise, in casual speech one hears such uses of verb particles (or adverbs) as full verbs in sentences such as "They upped the price." This switching of categories, which Leslie also does, offers some evidence that once a word is in the deep-structure lexicon, it is available for use in various ways. Furthermore, it appears that if a native speaker finds it natural to switch the usual category of a word (as switching the noun *blanket* to the verb *blanket*) another native speaker will understand him. As pointed out by Bever and Rosenbaum,[17] metaphorical uses of words can usually be recognized as regular lexical extensions of the 'literal' meanings of words.

It is as extensions of the usual meanings of words that Leslie seems to use 'Blanket me!' 'Paper me!' 'Apple me!', etc., for while other speakers of English have similarly extended the use of some of these nouns to their use as a verb, it is very doubtful that she has ever heard such models, certainly not the use of *apple* as a verb.

However, Leslie was not substituting her own noun or verb particle in every case for the reason that the adult model verb was not yet in her lexicon. For example, Leslie had /Ak/ 'take' in her active lexicon, but she didn't use it with *off*. She regularly used *up* and *down* as verbs, not just in these imperatives, but in other sentence types, such as,

I up a pen.   'I pick up a pen.'   (3;0)

While it may be assumed that, for Leslie, the meaning of her "Butter me!" approximates that of the speaker of "Butter me my blue," it cannot safely be assumed that both sentences are derived from similar underlying syntactic structures with certain deletions appearing in the surface structure of Leslie's imperative.

Both Brown, Cazden, and Bellugi-Klima[18] and Bloom[19] discuss the impossibility of knowing what the child's underlying form for the imperative may be. Brown et al. (p. 41) say, "Imperative sentences in adult grammar are derived by transformation out of underlying strings containing the morpheme *imp* and having *you* as subject and *will* as auxiliary. This analysis is motivated by such adult sentences as, *Go chase yourself* and *Come here, will you?* Neither reflexives (*yourself*) nor tags (*will you*) occurred in early child speech, and so the fact justifying the adult analysis were lacking."

We propose here that Leslie's productive use of the imperative sentence patterned after "Watch me!" is another of her strategies for first language acquisition. The sentence structure could hardly be simpler. It follows the open/pivot pattern discussed by Braine[20] with *me* as the constant pivot, and the open class readily taking in new vocabulary. This is a pattern that usually starts around eighteen months, or at the beginning of patterned speech, and because it does not coincide with the adult patterns, is dropped when the child develops more complex sentence structures. The imperative pattern discussed here differs, however, from the typical open/pivot patterned sentences; this pattern matches the adult model except for some of the lexical items admitted into the open class. It therefore constitutes a pattern that Leslie not only produced but heard regularly. While no count is available as to the number of times this imperative pattern was used in comparison to all other sentence types, it can safely be said that it was a frequent sentence pattern in Leslie's speech development up to age 3;0.

Notes

1. John Lyons, *Introduction to theoretical linguistics* (Cambridge, England: Cambridge University Press, 1969), p. 307.
2. Melissa Bowerman, *Early syntactic development* (London: Cambridge University Press, 1973), p. 149.
3. Lois Bloom, *Language development: Form and function in emerging grammars* (Cambridge, Mass.: M.I.T. Press, 1970).
4. Roger Brown, Courtney Cazden and Ursula Bellugi-Klima, "The child's grammar from I to III," in *Minnesota Symposia on Child Psychology,* vol. II, edited by J.P. Hill (Minneapolis: University of Minnesota Press, 1968), pp. 28-73.
5. M.A.K. Halliday, "Learning how to mean," in *Foundations of language development: A multidisciplinary approach,* edited by Eric and Elizabeth Lenneberg, UNESCO and IBRO, forthcoming.
6. David McNeill, *The acquisition of language* (New York: Harper and Row, 1970), pp. 20-21.
7. Bloom, *Language development.*

8. Werner F. Leopold, *Speech development of a bilingual child,* vol. 4 (Evanston, Ill.: Northwestern University Press, 1949).

9. Bloom, *Language development,* p.122.

10. Charles A. Ferguson, "Absence of copula and the notion of simplicity: A study of normal speech, baby talk, foreigner talk and pidgins," in *Social factors in pidginization and creolization,* edited by Dell Hymes (New York: Cambridge University Press, 1971).

11. Leopold, *Speech development of a bilingual child.*

12. Ursula Bellugi, "The acquisition of negation," Ph.D. dissertation, Harvard University, 1967.

13. J.L. Austin, *How to do things with words,* edited by J.O. Urmson (New York: Oxford University Press, 1962).

14. D. Terence Langendoen, *The study of syntax: The generative-transformational approach to the structure of American English* (New York: Holt, Rinehart and Winston, 1969), p. 123.

15. Ibid., p. 149.

16. Emmon Bach, "Nouns and noun phrases," in *Universals in linguistic theory,* edited by Emmon Bach and Robert T. Harms (New York: Holt, Rinehart and Winston, Inc., 1968), pp. 91-122.

17. Thomas G. Bever, and Peter S. Rosenbaum, "Some lexical structures and their empirical validity," in *Readings in English transformational grammar,* edited by R.A. Jacobs and P.S. Rosenbaum (Waltham, Mass.: Ginn and Co., 1970), pp. 3-20.

18. Brown, Cazden, and Bellugi-Klima, "The child's grammar from I to III."

19. Bloom, *Language development.*

20. Martin D.S. Braine, "The ontogeny of English phrase structure: The first phase," in *Child language: A book of readings,* edited by Aaron Bar-Adon and Werner F. Leopold (Englewood Cliffs, New Jersey: Prentice-Hall, 1971), pp. 279-89.

7
Development of Negation

As pointed out by Bellugi, "Negation is a universal concept for which all languages must find some means of expression."[1] It is also a concept for which children find some means of expression at a very early point in their language development. It would be a very unusual child who had not found a means of expressing negative feelings before any language, in the usual sense of the word, had been acquired.

Leopold observes that in the pre-speech period, the negative reaction is expressed by crying. At 1;3, Leopold reports that crying meant "I do not want to" in Hildegard's case: "the form of the utterance precludes all doubt as to its emotional character. This primitive reaction was not definitely replaced by the verbal negative until 1;6. From the beginning, the negative was sometimes used factually, as a statement; but the emotional and volitional implications prevailed until 1;11."[2]

At very early ages babies also learn to push away food, objects, or even individuals they don't want. At this point, the child has learned to express *rejection*, one of the three semantic categories of negation listed by Bloom which are used by young children. Bloom does not discuss these pre-linguistic expressions, however. The other two categories are *nonexistence* and *denial*.[3] Rejection appears to be the most primitive of these three in that it appears at the earliest age, although, as suggested above, in a manner that does not follow that of the adult language system.

Hebb, Lambert, and Tucker suggest that there are three aspects of negation which a child must master in the sense of comprehension, not production: prohibition by another person of some action by the child himself, absence or nonexistence of something familiar or expected, and denial (refusal) of something desired.[4] They suggest that prohibition is the simplest of these three: the prohibition is enforced by another person and the child, in the beginning, only needs to comprehend and respond. At a somewhat later time, the child may take the adult role in playing with dolls or pets and say 'no' in imitation of the adult in prohibiting the doll or pet from some activity. Hebb et al. do not specify the semantic category of rejection, nor does Bloom include a category that would encompass prohibition, as Hebb et al. describe it. Bloom was concerned with the types of negation found in production, not comprehension, and it appears that her three children did not engage in such role-playing during her observations. In observing Leslie, as well as Fred, John, and Gregory, it was found that the children engaged almost entirely in this kind of role-playing when they were not under close observation; they were heard to spank their dolls or tell them not to do something, but the children never directed this into a microphone.

Because of Leslie's late use of syntactic negation (see table 7-1), it has been found useful to adopt Halliday's classification of language development into three phases, the first of which consists of mastering "certain basic functions of language, each one having a small range of alternatives, or 'meaning potential,' associated with it."[5]

The following tentative system of the functions of language which develop during Phase I were suggested by Halliday (and briefly discussed in Chapter 3) in the approximate order in which they appear:

Instrumental	'I want'
Regulatory	'do as I tell you'
Interactional	'me and you'
Personal	'here I come'
Heuristic	'tell me why'
Imaginative	'let's pretend'
Informative	'I've got something to tell you'

All of these functions, with the possible exception of the last, appear, Halliday suggests, before the child makes the transition to the adult language system.

The first language function to appear, then, is the instrumental, 'I want' or 'I don't want.' (Any of the functions can appear as affirmative or negative, of course.) Although, as Halliday points out, in Phase I the expression of meaning owes nothing to the English language, and has no syntax, morphology or vocabulary intermediate between content and expression, the meanings do follow the adult semantic system. Due to this fact, the adult is able to respond to the child's early meanings even though their expression does not follow the adult linquistic system. Certaintly the adult does not wait for the child to say 'no' before he recognizes any negative meanings expressed by the child. The adult accepts gestures, shouting, and other forms of behavior to the extent that he understands them.

According to Halliday's ordering of language functions, *rejection*, which is included in *instrumental*, essentially as 'I don't want,' appears first, or among the first, functions of language. Hebb et al.'s category of prohibition would be included in Halliday's *regulatory* function, 'don't do that,' and also appears

Table 7-1
The Age of the Production of Negation by Eight Children

1	2	3	4	5	6
Child[a]	No First Used	Not First Used	Sentence Negative Element Invariant, Usually Initial or Final Position (Bellugi's Period A)	Negative Morpheme Internal in Sentence No Affirmative Aux. Verbs (Bellugi's Period B)	Exhibit a Mastery of Basic Sentence Negation Some Aspects of Tense & Number Agreement Used (Bellugi's Period C)
Leslie	1;4	2;10	2;4–3;2 (mean age, 2;9)	3;2–3;7 (mean, 3;4½)	3;8–4;0 (mean 3;10½)
Eve			1;7[b]	1;11	2;2
Adam			2;4	2;11	3;2
Sarah			2;5	3;0	3;8
Kathryn			1;9	2;0	
Eric			1;8	1;11	
Gia			1;11	2;3	
Hildegard	1;6	1;11	1;11–2;3	2;4–2;5	2;6–2;10
Anthony				2;4–2;6	

[a]Data on Adam, Eve, and Sarah is from Ursula Bellugi, "The acquisition of negation," Ph.D. dissertation, Harvard University, 1967; Kathryn, Eric, and Gia from Lois Booom, *Language Development: Form and Function in Emerging Grammars* (Cambridge, Mass.: M.I.T. Press, 1970); Hildegard from Werner F. Leopold, *Speech Development of a Bilingual Child*, 4 vols. (Evanston, Ill., Northwestern University Press, 1939–1949); and Anthony from Ruth Hirsch Weir, *Language in the Crib* (The Hague: Mouton and Co., 1962).

[b]Where only one age is listed in columns 4, 5, and 6, it is the mean age.

among the first functions of language. And, just as a child may get slapped on the hand for not responding when the parent says "No, don't do that," the child may also use a slapping or hitting gesture, but not use the verbal command.

Halliday points out, "From the functional point of view, as soon as there are meaningful expressions there is language, and the investigation can begin at a time before words and structures have evolved to take over the burden of realization. It then emerges that the child already has a linguistic system before he has any words or structures at all."[6]

Leopold has also noted that with Hildegard "meanings were always developed before sound-forms."[7] Most linguists would probably agree with this. The point of departure comes in calling expressions that do not include words and structure *language*, as Halliday does.

Because of Leslie's extended use of non-adult means of expressing negation, we deem it essential in this study to adopt Halliday's functional point of view. While Bloom did not go as far as Halliday does in admitting non-adult forms as expressions of meaning,[8] she did give attention to "semantic intent" in the language development of her children (perhaps because they were younger than the Harvard children were at the onset of the study), and admitted as negative statements those which included no negative morpheme, but were accompanied by head shaking, pushing an object away or refusing to follow a direction. She also observed at least three syntactically affirmative statements that appeared to occur with negative intent with Eric at Time II. Bellugi,[9] in her thorough study of the acquisition of negation in children, looked only at the syntactic aspects of the problem. She did, however, admit a small number of syntactically affirmative statements as negations because the parents of the child accepted them as such. In her study, she encountered comparatively few problems of understanding the child such as were found with Leslie because Brown and his colleagues at Harvard picked children "whose speech was largely intelligible, who had a high rate of production."[10]

Expression of Negation Without a Negative Morpheme

Leslie's earliest expressions of negation, aside from crying, as mentioned above, were rejecting food she didn't want or toys that were given to her but which she didn't want, by pushing them away or throwing them on the floor. At least through 1;9, on occasions such as when someone tried to take off a sweater or bib or any garment she wanted left on, or when someone tried to feed her and she wanted to feed herself, or when the dog tried to take something away from her, she jabbered in a loud voice with clipped sounds, such as 'baw-bawbaw' with no recognizable words. Along with this loud voice, she almost invariably used gestures such as a stiff, outstretched arm and clenched fist or pointing finger, and her head often bobbed in small jerks. She had begun to use 'no no' in appropriate ways at 1;4, but seemed to use it only in situations which did not arouse very strong emotions for her, as though words alone were insufficient for some occasions. These occasions seemed to arise frequently, a fact which is probably related to Leslie's own personality and those of her family members, none of whom would be described as placid.

There are many examples reported in which, after children have acquired a minimum amount of syntactic structure and have at least *no* in their lexicon, they make syntactically affirmative statements which carry a negative meaning. If the child uses a standard adult gesture, such as shaking his head while he makes the statement, the meaning is unmistakable. Leopold, for example, reports that Hildegard did this at 1;11, saying "Mary Alice's weh weh alle," with a shaking of her head, meaning Mary Alice has no pain any longer.[11] *Alle* was used in the sense of *all gone*, so perhaps does not truly qualify as an affirmative statement, from the child's point of view, since *alle* appeared to her to be serving as a negative morpheme. Leopold also reports that at 2;3 Hildegard omitted the negative in "Uh-uh, I want that," meaning 'I don't want that,' and in other cases in which no negative gestures were reported.[12]

Bloom reported a "unique 'stereotype' structure": "ə want any shoes," and two other sentences "ə find it" and "/jə/ find it," all of which appeared to occur with negative intent but without a negative morpheme in Eric's speech at Time II.[13]

In the first instance, *any* may have had a negative connotation for Eric inasmuch as this is the indefinite quantifier required in negative statements in standard English, whereas *some* is required for affirmative statements: *I don't want any*; *I want some.* *Some*, it should be noted, is the unmarked member of the pair *some/any*, is usually learned first, and often substitutes for *any* at this early stage. At 3;6 Leslie said

> I don't want some. 'I don't want any.'   (3;6)

even though *any* was in her lexicon at this point. Although *any* was not always used where it should be by adult standards, when it was used, it appeared to carry a negative connotation:

> Anybody have white hair.   Only you.   I don't have white
>   hair.   Daddy don't have white hair.   'No one has white
>   hair except you.'   (3;5)

> Anybody don't like me.   'No one likes me.'   (3;5)

> Anybody can't come in here.   'No one can come in here.'   (3;5)

Gregory also used positive statements with negative meaning. "My want

to," for example, was his usual say of saying "I don't want to" from at least
1;7 to 1;9. There would not have been any way for a stranger to know that
this was a negative statement, as it was not accompanied by head shaking or any
other gesture of negation. It was only through consistently negative behavior
on Gregory's part that the family learned this meaning.

How many more statements with negative meanings, but without negative
morphemes, children make without being understood as such can only be
speculated upon, but it may be that affirmative statements, being the unmarked
member of the pair, *affirmative/negative,* may very frequently be overgeneralized
to include negative meaning. This is in spite of the fact that the lexical pair,
yes/no, no is usually learned first, in our own experience and according to Jespersen[14] and Leopold.[15]

From 2;10. and perhaps earlier without having been understood as such,
through 4;7, Leslie used syntactically affirmative statements to express negative
meanings. Sometimes these carried paralinguistic features that indicated, at
least to family members, their negative nature, but often there was no apparent
clue to the negative meaning except context, either verbal or physical. Sometimes the omission may have been purely on phonetic grounds, e.g., the variation between *can* and *can't* (only *ca* with a nasalized *a* at early stages) which
continued from 2;10 through 4;4, at least, can be attributed to Leslie's tendency
to omit final consonants. If she had the intention to say *can't* but unintentionally produced only *can*, this would explain her failure to mark the statement as
negative in some other way, as was often the case.

Some of Leslie's syntactically affirmative statements that carried no paralinguistic features or gestures to indicate their negative nature, and are therefore
at least susceptible to analysis as an extension of the affirmative to include the
negative follows:

> /E/   know   'I don't know.'   (3;3)   This was used very often,
> both earlier and later than this time, and always with negative
> meaning.

> I hear!   I hear!   'I can't hear!'   (2;11)   The room was noisy
> and she covered her ears and yelled. She may have intended
> the gesture and the loud voice to be indicators of negation,
> but it was not clearly interpretable. Leslie made her meaning
> more clear by turning off the record player to lower the noise
> level.

> No...   mama turn!   My turn!   'I don't want you to do it. I
> want to do it myself.'   (3;0)

> No!   My dress...my dress off!   I don't want my dress off.'   (2;11)

Bloom discusses sentences produced by her three subjects which had an
initial *no* and were followed by affirmative sentences.[16] With her children
(Times II-V, ages 1;10 to 2;1) the *no* in each instance was anaphoric and did
not apply to the remainder of the sentence. In the examples above, the *no*
is anaphoric in that it refers to the action of someone who was trying to help
her open a gift at her third birthday party or take her dress off, but the syntactically affirmative sentence carried a negative meaning.

Another example without a negative morpheme:

/A A gEkIn pUsh E wont/

> (this kind purse want)   'I don't want the box in my purse.'
> (3;0) She took a tiny box from her purse and handed it
> to the investigator, making her meaning clear.

Leslie may have been making use of something which she considered to be an
indication of negation, but which was missed by the investigator, as well as by
family members, who reported frequent use of syntactically affirmative statements with negative meanings, in which the non-linguistic context was their
clue to her meaning.

It should be noted that these examples from Leslie's speech were from
ages 2;11 to 3;3, whereas Eric at Time II was 1;8, Gregory was 1;7 to 1;9, and
Hildegard was 1;11 when similar instances were noted in their speech development.

Negative Meanings Indicated by Paralinguistic
Features and Gestures

There were a variety of strategies that Leslie used to express negative
meaning. In the examples that follow, her meaning would have been missed
by strangers, and family members may have missed some, but it is clear that
she was signaling the negative meaning in her own way—she was not extending
the affirmative statement to include negative meaning.

In the first pair of examples, she appeared to have been using two strategies: the use of two adjoining, contrastive statements, one applying to one
person, the next applying to another, and the use of contrasting intonation
patterns.

> /I ə ikE nO*th* fwe ə ikE nO*th*/ 'I don't have an ikky nose.
> Fred has an ikky nose.' (2;11) She had said something, the
> only understandable word of which was *nose*, and was asked,
> "Do you need to blow your nose?" She was replying that she
> didn't need to, but Fred did.

The stress was on the first word of each sentence, but whereas the final word
of the first sentence (the one with negative meaning) did not have a rising intonation, the final word of the second sentence did rise.

Another example using contrastive pattern:

> Oh oh!   Gog feet sticking out!   Boy feet sticking out.
> 'The dog's feet are sticking.   The boy's feet are not.'
> (3;1) She was looking at a picture book, and the boy
> and a dog were in bed together.

In this case, the rising intonation was on the final word of the first sentence, and
the second sentence (the one with negative meaning) did not have rising intonation. With the exception of the initial noun of each negative sentence, everything
(/ ə ikE *nOth*/ and *sticking out*) had a low intonation pattern. A final rising
intonation was on the affirmative sentence of each pair.

The following pair of sentences does not follow quite the same pattern, but
the contrast remains:

> Fred Gikky Mouse wash.   I a /rE rE wosh/   'Fred has a
> Mickey Mouse watch. I have a real, real watch.'   (2;10)

In this instance, the second statement, the negative one, carried not only a steadily
lowering pitch, but she lowered her head as the sentence progressed so that her
chin was almost to her chest by the time she was finished, a gesture Leslie frequently used with negation. Her eyes were opened wider than usual, a gestural
aspect of negation not unusual in adults, particularly when addressing children,
though perhaps most often used in warning or prohibition situations, e.g., "I
don't think you should do that!" The additional lowering of her head on the
second sentence may have been to compensate for the affirmative nature of the
statement. In the sentences about the noses and the feet sticking out, the negative sentence merely omitted the negative morpheme: 'Boy feet *not* sticking
out,' for example, would have made it the usual negation for a child. The same
could not be done with 'I have a real watch.' From the adult point of view,
one might say the pair of sentences could be translated 'Fred's watch is phony,
mine is real,' but her intonation pattern indicates her syntactic pattern is 'Fred's
is a Mickey Mouse watch; mine is not.'

The next group of sentences were a series in a conversation while Leslie
was looking at two different books with pictures of animals in them. While
they don't offer the same kind of contrast that the above pairs do, her addition
of "They love me," seems as though it may have been added, in part, to serve
this purpose.

> /A be. . . E beg hUrt mE   A O mE/   'Ladybugs won't hurt
> me. They love me.'   (3;0)   /Ebeg/   is Leslie's usual way

of saying *ladybug* so the change from /A beg/ to /E beg/
represents a self-correction of the pronunciation.

/A wrn...A wrn E ker mE/ 'The worm doesn't scare me.'
(3;0) Again, she appeared to be attempting to correct her
production of *the worm*, but the second attempt was just
like the first, as nearly as could be discerned.

This sentence didn't offer a contrast, but since Leslie used a strong stress as
well as falling intonation on *me*, she may have considered that these two markers
signaled the negation. The investigator asked, then, partly to be certain of her
meaning, "Don't worms scare you?" She answered,

/nO A O mE/ 'No, they love me.' (3;0)

As the conversation continued, she used the following sentences:

/E ylən E ger mE/ 'The lion doesn't scare me.'

/E horth E ger mE/ 'The horse doesn't scare me.'

/E mauth E ger mE/ 'The mouse doesn't scare me.'

The explanatory (or contrastive) 'They love me,' was not added to these successive statements, perhaps because it was clear that she was being understood.
These statements were not in immediate succession, but all within the same
conversation, several minutes apart. In each case, the /E ger mE/ carried a
falling intonation, as is typical of her negations.
About two weeks later in a conversation regarding water, Leslie said,

/E gerd/ 'I'm not scared.' (3;0) This carried the falling
intonation, but no contrastive sentence, nor any noticeable
gesture of negation.

Leslie had been asked if she would sing "Twinkle, Twinkle Little Star"
and she said,

·No, I can. I /U u E gU e E o pE kU or A eth pE kU or/

(No, I can't I u   e   p   q   r   a   s   p   q   r)
'No, I can't, but I can say the letters of the alphabet.' (2;10)
She often used this tactic; if she were asked to do something
she either couldn't do or didn't want to do, she would offer to
do or say something else, e.g., she was asked, "Can you say

mother?" She answered, "No, I can't. . .I say butterfy!"
(2;10)

The request was repeated in case she had misunderstood. This time she said,

/E gE kE gI dor nau/   'I'm not goin to sing 'Twinkle Twinkle
Little Star' now.'   (2;10)   While this sentence had falling
intonation as well as lowering of volume, there were no unmistakable clues as to the negation of the sentence, and she was
asked again, "Are you going to sing it now?"

/nO   I van gE kE kI gor a mE hOm/   'No!   I want to sing
'Twinkle Twinkle Little Star' at my home.'   (2;10)   An example
of an anaphoric *no* followed by an affirmative sentence.

It should be noted here that the falling intonation pattern referred to in
connection with Leslie's negated sentences appears to be slightly different than
the falling intonation used for affirmative statements. In Leslie's negated
sentences, the intonation falls steadily, following the subject, if there is one.
In her affirmative sentences, the falling intonation is on the final phoneme,
final syllable of the word, or the entire final word of a sentence. We have been
unable to locate a comprehensive study of adult intonation patterns for similar
positive/negative sentence types, so are unable to say how 'standard' this intonation pattern may be. From casual observation it would not seem to be ab-
normal, anyway. However, even if these patterns are followed by adults, a
negative morpheme is also used as the principal mark of negation. It is not surprising, therefore, that the intonation pattern as the principal signal for negation
was often missed by family members, and Leslie was misunderstood.

Another instance of a contrastive intonation pattern is reported by Miller
and Ervin in the disambiguation of two-word utterances by intonation in sentences such as *CHRISTY room* (possessive) and *Christy ROOM* (locative).[17]

Leopold reported that Hildegard practiced contrasting positive and negative sentences, such as "Miau da, Miau not da," 'Meow, or cat, there. Meow
not there' starting at 1;11.[18] He pointed out that the negative morpheme was
stressed in the second statement, and the adverb of place was stressed and was
given added length in the first statement, but unstressed and not so long in
the second. Leopold quotes Synder as saying that contrastive statements of
the kind "Not dat boat hot; dat boat hot," (also in reverse order) are typical
of age 2;6.[19] While Leslie used this contrastive pattern at a later age than
reported by Leopold, and she omitted the negative morpheme, she followed a
common pattern in practicing negative/positive sentence formations.

Lord reported that a 24-month old child, Jennifer, used a rising intonation
to indicate negation, e.g., "I wan' put it on!" where *I* is normal intonation
level, and the remainder of the sentence is higher, except for a final brief fall

at the end.[20] Other examples she offered, with similar intonation patterns, and all with negative intention, were: "I want need help!" "Like, like it!" Two sentences, identical except for intonation pattern, offer a neat contrast here. "Read it!" where both words are high pitch carries negative meaning, but "Read it!" where *read* is high and *it* is low (normal) pitch, means "*I* want to read it!" At this age, Jennifer had *no* in her lexicon, and used it independently, but it was never attached to a sentence. This was a brief stage for Jennifer, however; by 25 months she was using *no, not, don't*, and *can't* in sentence initial position with or without a verb following.

The fact that Leslie used a low, or falling intonation pattern for negation and Jennifer used a high, or rising intonation pattern for the same function, may depend on the patterns associated with negation that each child heard most frequently. Either pattern is possible in adult speech.

Negative Meanings Without Negative Morphemes or Paralinguistic Markers

While no paralinguistic markers of negation were noted in the sentences below, they are all short and may have contained Leslie's negative intonation marker, but were not detected because of their shortness.

As was mentioned above, Leslie frequently omitted the final *t* of *can't*, leaving the negative and affirmative words identical phonetically. However, there is no reason to assume that this represents an extension of the affirmative to include the negative meaning, inasmuch as she omitted final consonants on many words. If this omission caused a misunderstanding, she often repeated the *I can* by saying *I can't* in a louder voice.

Other examples of negative meaning without the negative morpheme follow:

> /an/   did it. 'I didn't do it.'   (3;5)   To clarify her meaning, the investigator asked, "You didn't do it?" She answered,

> No.   Somebody else.   (3;5)

> /dOim yAk/ 'It's not a lake.'   (3;0)   Exactly what the first word represents to Leslie is not clear, but her meaning was that the picture she was looking at was of *water* not of a *lake*.

> /E not rEdit...A nE rEdit/ 'Don't read it.'   (3;2)   The second instance represents a self-correction, it seems. The standard *not* was changed to /nE/, perhaps unintentionally, but it appeared to represent the negative morpheme to her.

The negative meaning in these three examples was clear; Leslie's lexical intentions were not so clear. It can be assumed in each case that she was trying to produce some standard negative morpheme, but what was actually produced in each instance was a nasal to serve as the mark of negation.

The principal negative morphemes in English have an initial *n*: *no, not,* and *never,* and most negative prefixes include a nasal: *un-, in-* and *im-*. Jespersen comments on the use by little children of /nenenene/ as a natural expression of fretfulness and discomfort; so natural, in fact, that it doesn't need to be learned.[21] Statements of complaint by children have also been noted as being nasalized.[22] Leslie's use of the nasal in this way is interesting in view of her propensity to rely on vowels (see Chapter 4). In this instance, she is not relying on the /O/ of *no* or the /o/ of *not*, but has selected the initial consonant.

The final consonant was omitted from contracted negations, not consistently, but often:

Well, I don' do it like that.   (4;4)

It doesn' matter.   (4;4)

I won' tell.   (3;0)

When she was using the same negative forms for emphasis, she not only included the final consonant, but gave a word boundary to the contracted negative morpheme, always with /unt/ rather than not.

Well, you did+unt say that.   (4;4)

I did+unt know what to do.   (4;1)

I wanted to tell Mommy something and I could+unt.   (4;1)

In the following example at 4;7, it is impossible to know why the negative morpheme was not present with *could* inasmuch as Leslie had started using *couldn't* by 4;0, but her meaning was clearly negative:

They could have a house cause all the houses were use up, so
    they just said "Boo hoo, boo hoo" cause they wanted a
    house, but suddenly they saw a tent.   (4;7)

**Earliest Stage of Negation Reported in
Other Studies**

Bellugi discusses the negative utterances of the three Harvard children during what she calls Period A, the first period of her study.[23] At this time the mean age of each child for the period was: Eve, 1;7, Adam, 2;4, and Sarah, 2;5. The negative sentences they produced at this time were limited in structure, consisting largely of nouns and verbs without indication of tense or number. There were no auxiliary verbs and the negative morpheme, either *no* or *not*, was usually in either initial or final position in the sentence, as follows:

No. . .wipe finger

More. . . no

No a boy bed

No singing song

No money

No sit there

Wear mitten no

Not a teddy bear

No fall!

No mommy read

Bellugi based her analysis for Period A on ten hours of speech per child; subsequent periods are based on six hours of speech for each child.[24] During this ten-hour period, the three children exhibited great individual differences in the quantity, if not the quality, of negative production. Eve produced only seven utterances that were categorized as negations; two of these, *Man (no) spoon*, and *Man (no) taste it*, apparently omitted the negative morpheme in the production. Sarah produced 14 negative sentences, and Adam produced 64. Of these three groups of examples, only Adam's contained such non-adult sounding structures as *No go back, Up no?* and *No a boy bed*. Most of the negative sentences produced by all of the children followed possible adult syntax, such as *No string*, even though the meaning may have differed somewhat from what adult meaning might have been for a similar utterance.

The three children in Bloom's study reached a comparable stage of development of negation at different times: Kathryn at Time I (1;9), Eric at Time

II (1;8), and Gia at Time IV (1;11). Examples of their negative utterances during this period follow:

No pocket

No dirty soap

No more juice

No open the wallet

Not here.

Between the ages of 2;4 and 2;6, Anthony used the following negative sentences:[25]

Not, that's little book

Is not black

Mommy is not home

Bobo's not throwing

Don't go on the desk

Don't touch Mommy Daddy's desk

Don't take the glasses off.

These sentences indicate that Anthony would probably be in Period B at this age. Individual differences among children in rate of development at very early ages is great. Leslie went through an exceptionally long period of initial syntactic development in negation, just as she did in other areas. From 1;4 through 2;10 there were numerous examples of her shouting 'no no no no no, gagi' to the dog, 'No, mine,' or just a series of 'no no's' to anyone, accompanied by the behavior described earlier in this chapter. The first sentences beyond this pattern that included a negative morpheme were recorded at 2;4.

Using Bellugi's criteria for periods of development of negation, it was hard to find clear indications as to when a new stage of development had taken place. However, beginning at 3;2 Leslie began to use negative sentences such as:

I need this side not crack. 'I don't like it that this block
   is cracked.'   (3;2)

My daddy don't have one. (3;2)

These negations seemed to be beyond the Period A type negations in which
there were no auxiliary verbs and the negative morpheme was positioned either
initially or finally in a two- or three-word sentence. Therefore, in order to try
to compare Leslie with the Bellugi children, 3;1 has been set as the end of her
Period A in negations and 3;2 as the beginning of Period B.

It will be noted from the list that follows of negative sentences in Period A
that most of them can be categorized as denials, as opposed to rejection or
nonexistence. As discussed earlier, rejection was expressed very frequently but
without the use of negative morphemes. Nonexistence did not seem to be a
very important semantic category for Leslie. It may be that she tried to express
it and was misunderstood.

The list that follows does not include all of Leslie's negative utterances
during the period from 2;4 through 3;1, but offers examples of every type
of negation she used.

/nO. . .hi ə br/   'No, him a boy.'   (2;4)

/nO. . .I ə babin ə wI/   'No, I'm going for a wagon ride.   (2;6)

/nO. . .mI bI/   'No, it's my bike.'   (2;6)

/nO. . .mI drn/   'No, it's my turn.'   (2;6)

Oh, no!   My mamma /wI/   'Oh, no, my grandpa's outside.'   (2;7)

These five sentences are examples of the anaphoric negation and an affirmative
sentence and was a frequent pattern for Leslie for two or three years. From
about 2;4 to 2;10 there are many examples of a transcribed *no* followed by a
string of words, sometimes they could be glossed and sometimes they couldn't:

/nO I wu mI ə wudu de wA/   (Meaning unknown.)   (2;6)

No /E/ not!   (2;10)   This was Leslie's first use of *not* according
to family members and to transcriptions. She was playing with
a balloon and the investigator said it would make a loud noise
on the tape if she broke it. This was her emphatic reply.

No, I not!   (2;11)

No, Mommy not. 'Mommy didn't make my bedspread.'   (2;11)

She was asked, "Are you Leslie?" and answered,

No.   /ko/   baby.   'No.   Call me baby.'   (2;11)

Leslie was conversing about a picture in a story book:

/gEkIn woyr/   'This kind is water.'   (3;0)   The investigator
said, "Yes, there's some water. There's a nice little lake."

/nO. . .E yAk   E woyr/   'No, it's not a lake. It's water.'

The investigator replied, "It's water.   Um hum."

/dOim yAk/   The first word could not be glossed, but it was
apparent Leslie was reasserting that it was *not* a lake. She was
familiar with the word *water*, but *lake* was apparently a new
lexical item.

Leslie was in an argumentative mood during this session, and as the story
progressed, the investigator mentioned that something looked like a tree.

/nO ə twE/   'Not a tree.'   (3;0)   The investigator asked,
"Oh, what is it?"

/gEkI ə twE/   'This kind is a tree.'   (3;0) She pointed to
a more realistically drawn tree.

The story continued: "There were sure to be foxes in the woods or turtles
in the water and she was not about to raise her family . . . "

/nO. . . no foks E wIr   duk*th* fim E wIr/   'No, not foxes in
water. Ducks swim in water.'   (3;0)   *Woods* was probably
unfamiliar to her, and she confused it with *water*.

I won' tell.   (3;0)

/I mer ə wEd *th*ith   I kant/   (3;0)

(I   read this   I can't)   The first part of the utterance is
not glossable word by word, but the gist of it was "I tried to
read this but I can't (or couldn't)."   She had been looking
at a book, pretending to read it, and handed it to the investigator to read.

I don't hear anything.   (3;1)

Leslie was asked "What's this animal?"

/notmau/   A giraffe.   'Not an animal.   It's a giraffe.'   (3;1)

There are a number of ways in which the negative sentences of Leslie's Period A do not seem to be equivalent to the Period A sentences of Bellugi's and Bloom's children. The first is the prevalence of negative meaning without a negative morpheme, as illustrated above. The second is Leslie's syntax, which is so idiosyncratic at times that even the insertion of the negative morpheme would not make it easily understandable.

Later Periods of Negation

In stages of development beyond Bellugi's Period A, Leslie's development of negation does not differ much more from that of the children discussed above than they differ from each other. Leslie's Period B could be said to extend from 3;2 to 3;7 (mean of 3;4½). Eve's mean age for this time period was 1;11, Adam's was 2;11, and Sarah's 3;0. During this period of development, according to Bellugi, the negative morpheme is positioned internally in the sentence and has a greater variety of forms, including *no, not, don't,* and *can't*; the latter two are restricted to occurrences with nonprogressive main verbs.

Examples of Leslie's negative sentences during this period follow:

These are not two green blocks! No. Two pink ones.   (3;2)

This not going in the water. Right?   (3;4)   This is her first
    noted attempt at a tag question, and she used the invariable
    form, which is often used by children.

These same? Not. No, one's a little wider.   Um, /A/ not a
    same. One belongs green. One belongs blue.   (3;2)

/E/   not read it.   Now read it.   'Stop reading.   Now read.'   (3;2)

I don't have a new one.   (3;3)

My feet don't have sand in.   'There's no sand in my sox.'   (3;3)

You can't know.   'I'm not going to tell you.'   (3;4)

You can't /ə baf ə mE cu/ you too big!   'You can't take a
    bath with me because you're too big.'   (3;4)

Can't take a helmet off.   Only Freds can.   (3;6)

I can't hear you, either   (3;4)

This not a shoe, either.   (3;4)

You not nice, either.   (3;5)

Just as *any* must be used with negation and *some* with affirmative, so *either* is used with negation and *too* with the affirmative. The examples above, at 3;4, are the first transcribed use of *either*, and her use of *too* was first recorded at 3;7. No misuses of either word have been observed. Sarah was first noted using *either* in Period E (mean age for period, 4;6) and Adam in Period D (3;6). This is one of the few instances in which Leslie produced a form earlier than Sarah or Adam.

My father not told you. 'My father told you not to.'   (3;3)

The investigator answered that her father had told her to take the dog, and she answered,

My father not take it, cuz is breakable!   (Breakable = hands off!)

This appears to be an example of a need for embedding sentences, but Leslie is not able to do it yet, so must express the idea, "My father didn't tell you to take the dog" in two separate sentences, leaving the meaning unclear.

That is not good.   That yukky.   (3;7)

My not wearing my slip. Cause it's too hot.   (3;7)

Elephants got trunks.   Not ducks.   Cep this duck do.   (3;7)

Not finished yet.   (3;7)

We don't have Christmas lights, we don't.   You do?   (3;7)

Up to this time, the only tag question Leslie had used was *right*? This seems as though she has heard tag questions and is trying to pattern her sentence after them. The pitch and volume of *we don't* carried no hint of its use as an emphasis, which might be suggested by the syntax. Semantically, she didn't require a tag question, so one can only speculate about the syntactic form of the utterance. *You do?* is of course, a question, the order of which should have been reversed (see Chapter 8).   Leslie waited for a reply.

Anybody don't like me.   (3;5)

Anybody can't come in here.   (3;5)

Anybody have white hair.   Only you.   I don't have white hair.
Daddy don't have white hair.   (3;5)

I don't want some.   (3;6)

This not fit any more.   (3;7)

Leslie had not mastered the *some/any* or *any/no* rules at this point. As was mentioned above, *any* may carry a connotation of negation for her since she used it (in conjunction with *body*) without a negative morpheme. However, she proceeds to explain her meaning in that instance, and she does use a negative morpheme with *anybody* in other instances during this same time period. In the examples above, there are no exceptions to the rule she is discussing: *no one* likes her, and *no one* can come in. In the case of the white hair, there is an exception, which may explain her omission of the negative morpheme.

The first example of *didn't* was found at the end of this time period:

Cause I didn't want to do why xxxxx getting my letter.
(3;7)   The x's represent the portion of the utterance
that couldn't be glossed, but the portion that could be
indicates she was using *didn't* correctly.

Bellugi's Period C, the time at which a child exhibits a mastery of basic sentence negation, could be said to start for Leslie at 3;8 and continue through 4;0. Eve's mean age for this time period was 2;2, Adam's was 3;2 and Sarah's was 3;8.

Portions of one lengthy conversation at 3;11 about sparks, one of Leslie's favorite topics at this age, offers examples of her use of negation during this period. (The investigator's portion of the conversation is in quotations on the right.)

"And what did you say a spark was?"

ə   don't walk.

"What?"

Don't walk and don't say anything.

"They don't walk and they don't say anything?"

Huh um.   Don't have an eye or a nose.

"How else would you know a spark?"

It didn't have a head or anything, not two arms, not a tail. A spark
    was one of a thing of a xxxxxx don't walk on a wall or anything,
    or get in your houses. . .they jest be yellow sparks on a wall,
    cause don't have anyplace in em. . .don't have any places in em.
    Them don't eat anything and don't have anybody ə talk with,
    uh, . . .have things ə eat.

It appeared that the only way Leslie could describe sparks was to enumerate
what they didn't have or couldn't do. The passage illustrates her correct placement of the negative morpheme within the sentence, and also her correct usage
of *anybody, anything,* and *any place.* While there are many conjoined sentences, there are no embedded sentences using negation. The proper placement
of negation in embedded sentences is an indication of the beginning of Period D,
according to Bellugi. Sarah's mean age during this period was 4;2 and Adam's
was 3;6. Eve had left the program. Leslie entered this phase at 4;1 with sentences such as:

I did+unt know what to do.   (4;1)

I wanted to tell Mommy sumping and I could+unt.   (4;1)

At 4;1 Leslie was also using the negative form *never*:

Fred never kiss me!   (4;1)

Sparks never do anything.   (4;1)

Sarah had begun to use *never* during Period C, however Eve and Adam had not.
Adam started using *never* during Period D, often as part of a double negative,
of which he made frequent use. No examples of double negation are found in
Leslie's speech.

Discussion

Aside from her slowness in acquiring negation during the earliest periods of
time, the principal differences in Leslie's development of negation and that of
other children with whom she has been compared was her extensive reliance on
paralinguistic and gestural signals of negation during the early period of

development. The lowering intonation as well as lowering of volume were noted regularly in listening to her in person or in transcribing the tapes. Gestural features such as lowering her head or widening her eyes may have been used much more frequently than were noted because the investigator was listening more carefully than watching. Video taping would have been the ideal means of monitoring a child such as Leslie.

It may be seen that by the time Leslie was into Period B, her development of negation was very similar to that of the children with whom she was being compared, although she was somewhat older than the other children during any given period. By the time the study was concluded, it could be said that Leslie's use of negation was completely normal; her syntactic use of negation had started slowly, but she had caught up.

Notes

1. Ursula Bellugi, "The acquisition of negation," Ph.D. dissertation, Harvard University, 1967.
2. Werner F. Leopold, *Speech development of a bilingual child,* vol. 3 (Evanston, Ill.: Northwestern University Press, 1949), p. 7.
3. Lois Bloom, *Language development: Form and function in emerging grammars* (Cambridge, Mass.: M.I.T. Press, 1970), p. 173.
4. D.O. Hebb, W.E. Lambert, and G. Richard Tucker, "Language, thought and experience," *Modern Language Journal* 54 (1971): 212-22.
5. M.A.K. Halliday, "Learning how to mean," in *Foundations of language development: A multidisciplinary approach,* edited by Eric and Elizabeth Lenneberg, UNESCO and IBRO, forthcoming.
6. Ibid.
7. Werner F. Leopold, *Speech development of a bilingual child,* vol. 1 (Evanston, Ill.: Northwestern University Press, 1939), p. 22.
8. Bloom, *Language development.*
9. Bellugi, "The acquisition of negation."
10. Ibid., p. 3.
11. Leopold, *Speech development of a bilingual child,* vol. 1 (Evanston, Ill.: Northwestern University Press, 1939), p. 13.
12. Ibid., vol. 4, p. 16.
13. Bloom, *Language development,* p. 180.
14. Otto Jespersen, *Language, its nature, development and origin* (New York: W.W. Norton, 1922), p. 136.
15. Leopold, *Speech development of a bilingual child,* vol. 1, p. 112.
16. Bloom, *Language development,* pp. 160-61.
17. Wick Miller, and Susan M. Ervin, "The development of grammar in child language," in *The acquisition of language,* edited by Ursula Bellugi and

Roger Brown, Monographs of the Society for Research in Child Development, vol. 29, No. 1, 1964, pp. 9-34.

18. Werner F. Leopold, *Speech development of a bilingual child,* vol. 4 (Evanston, Ill.: Northwestern University Press, 1949), p. 44.

19. Alice D. Snyder, "Notes on the talk of a two-and-a-half year old boy," *Pegagogical Seminary* 21 (1914):412-24.

20. Carol Lord, "Variations in the pattern of acquisition of negation," paper read at the Sixth Annual Child Language Research Forum, April 6, 1974, at Stanford University, Stanford, California.

21. Jesperson, *Language, its nature, development and origin,* p. 136.

22. Thelma E. Weeks, "Speech registers in young children," *Child Development* 42 (1971):1119-31.

23. Bellugi, "The acquisition of negation."

24. Ibid, p. 6.

25. Ruth Hirsh Weir, *Language in the crib* (The Hague: Mouton and Co., 1962).

8 Development of Questions

One of the popular generalizations about speech behavior is that bright children ask many questions—it is an indication of curiosity and curiosity is an indication of intelligence.

Leslie has never asked many questions.[a] One could not characterize her as a non-curious child, but verbal questions did not give one much of a clue regarding her curiosity. However, Leslie did display her curiosity regarding her immediate surroundings by investigating anything within reach, touching and manipulating objects.

In observing Leslie, one was often struck by the thought that she must have had unspoken questions. She often gave one a long, steady, questioning look in situations where Fred would have asked a question immediately. Whether or not questions really did come to her mind, and if they did, whether she did not ask them because she was unable to formulate the question, or because early attempts to use questions were unsuccessful in getting answers, or whether she failed to ask questions for some other reason, cannot be known. However, the contrast between the number of questions Fred asked and the number Leslie asked at any comparable age was dramatic, and was a cause for concern by Leslie's parents.

Fred was an inveterate question-asker, the stereotyped bright child who kept his mother busy answering all sorts of questions, answerable and unanswerable. His first two-word questions started at 1;6. At 2;5 Fred asked the following questions (among many others):

> "Shall we have a pencil?" A polite form learned from his mother, meaning 'May I have a pencil?' His mother's questions, such as "Shall we take a nap now?" (rather than the more demanding "It's time for you to take your nap now!") used the inclusive *we* but referred just to Fred, as a rule. Fred used this *shall we* form frequently. Leslie has never been noted using it, though her mother used it with her just as she did with Fred.

---

[a]It is interesting to note that Morehead and Ingram observe that aphasic children who have been studied at the Institute for Childhood Aphasia, Stanford University, ask fewer questions than normal children even when the children are matched on the basis of length of utterance.[1] Aphasic children (as reported by Eisenson[2]) usually have more difficulty in processing auditory stimuli then visual stimuli, but to a greater degree than Leslie demonstrated.

"Are there going to be two repairmen?"

"It's chilly today, isn't it?" This was the earliest noted use of a
tag question by Fred (discussed further in Chapter 3).

By comparison, Leslie's earliest tag questions were:

We don't have Christmas lights, we don't. You do?   (3;7)

Those boots are big, are them?   (3;9)

More of Fred's questions at 2;5:

"Did you give me this pencil?"

"Did the mother take away my eggs?" *The mother* referred to
the waitress in the restaurant, representing one of Fred's
semantic overgeneralizations—any woman was a 'mother.'
The past tense of *do*, however, was present and was positioned
as in adult speech.

Leslie's earliest questions that could be interpreted as *do* questions appeared
at 3;1:

See Fred's teddy bear? 'Do you want to see Fred's teddy bear?'
(3;1) She was offering to go into Fred's room and bring
the teddy bear out for viewing.

See this? A bear. ə know I had one? 'Did you know I had
one?'   (3;1)

You have these? 'Do you have some of these?'   (3;4)

All of these questions relied on question intonation; none had the required preposed auxiliary verb (interrogative reversals), which Fred used invariably long
before this time.

Leslie's Earliest Questions

As is the usual case in language acquisition, Leslie's earliest questions relied
on intonation and the context, both linguistic and non-linguistic, for interpretation. Leslie's earliest monoremes could often be interpreted as questions: if she

heard a car in the driveway, she would ask 'Dada?" 'Is that Daddy driving up in the driveway?' Or if her mother was not in sight, she would say to another person in the room "Mama?" 'Where is Mommy?'

Many early questions were asked that were not as easily interpreted as these. A question intonation included in early, non-interpretable speech forms often left the listener with a helpless feeling. There was no way to answer the question, not being able to understand it, and questions seemed to be more difficult for Leslie to restate. In requests, for example, it was not unusual for Leslie to take a person by the hand and show him what she was talking about: go to the kitchen and point to a box of cereal, go to the record player and pick up a record, etc. Questions are more difficult to illustrate with gestures. Sometimes she tried:

/E mI gEgo/? (?)   (2;6)   It was a question, indicated by rising intonation. The investigator asked "What's your giga?" Leslie answered,

/O mI gEgo i mE/   'Oh, my giga is me.'   She touched her own cheek as she said it. The investigator asked, "Your face?" She answered,

/ə gEgo mI/   'A giga mine.'   (perhaps)

The explanations were not very illuminating. However, Leslie remained patient throughout this explanation. Often she became frustrated and impatient when others could not understand her. Perhaps this question was not very important to her.

Another example of a non-interpretable question:

/A mIk kU mI wrsh mI wE/? (?)   (2;10)   The intonation pattern indicated it was a question, but it could not be interpreted. The investigator asked for clarification, but was still unable to understand the question. After a slight pause, Leslie went on talking.

"Know-what?" Questions

Leslie's most frequently asked question was "Know what?" Syntactically, this is a question. Semantically, it was a means of getting attention. As soon as the listener said "No. What?" Leslie proceeded to say whatever she wanted to say. Perhaps she had learned by experience that she had a better chance of being understood if she could obtain the listener's attention before she started to talk.

The "Know-what?" question had several forms:

> I make? 'Do you know what I'm making?' (3;0)

> /I yIk/? 'Do you know what I like?' (3;4)

> /i *th*ith kod/? 'Do you know what this is called?' (3;5)
>   This was not a request for information. Leslie was waiting
>   to tell what she called it.

> You know what I call my trumpent? (4;1)

At the earliest stages of speech development, a name in question intonation often served this same function (Halliday's 'interactional' function[3]): Leslie would say "Mommy?" and as soon as her mother answered with "What?" or "Yes?" Leslie would say what she had to say, e.g.,

> Do mine. (2;2) Or,

> Mommy? Birds. A giga birds. (2;2) (No one was able to
>   assign a meaning to her word *giga*.)

At later ages (4;0 and on) she often used the form *know what*? without waiting for an answer. It served as an attention-getting introduction to a statement:

> Know what? Once I saw a monkey at the zoo hanging with his
>   two foots on a tree. (4;7)

> Know what /gUkE kurachr/ say one more K word is. . .kruddy.
>   'Do you know what the cookie monster (on Sesame Street)
>   says one more K word (a word that starts with *k*) is? Cruddy.'
>   (4;1) As the conversation continued, it was clear she was
>   referring to *karate*, but she had also heard the word *cruddy*
>   and had confused them.

> Know what? Jo in a Young's house. Know what? Her got
>   brown eyes. (4;2)

Wh Questions

Questions that use the interrogative words *what, where, when, why, who,* and *how* have been referred to as *wh* questions, particularly in child language

studies. There are a number of studies that report the development of these
(and other) questions in young children: Bellugi,[4] Bowerman,[5] Brown,[6]
Brown, Cazden, and Bellugi-Klima,[7] Gruber,[8] Klima and Bellugi,[9] Leopold,[10]
and Miller and Ervin,[11] and we will not attempt a review here.

Ervin-Tripp points out, "Since short-time storage is a prerequisite to building up long-term information about language, there will be prior acquisition of
contrasts of the following types: . . . d) Sentence-initial fixed-position forms
should be learned more easily than material in the middle of utterances. In
English, question words are learned very easily."[12] This appears to be true with
other children reported in diaries and child languages studies, but was not true
of Leslie (see table 8-1).

Leslie does, however, follow Ervin-Tripp's prediction that the highest
probability of retention in short-term storage will be the most recent material.[13]
Ervin-Tripp was referring, we assume, to retention of material heard by the
child, not produced by the child. However, in the examples that follow, Leslie
repeated only the most recent material of her own, almost as though she didn't
remember herself all of what she had said. It was the usual case that when
Leslie was misunderstood and was asked to repeat what she had just said, rather
than repeating the entire sentence, she would repeat just the final portion of it:

> /E. . .bOi E gU gub E bU bog/   (?)   (2;11)   The investigator
> could gloss only two of the words in the utterance, and asked
> "Hmm?"   Leslie repeated,

> /bUkth/ 'box'   She repeated just the last word of her utterance.

And again,

> /E mIk kU mI wrsh mI wE/   (?)   (2;11)   The investigator
> asked "Hmm?" and Leslie repeated.

> /mI wish/   (?)   This time she repeated the last two words, which
> in turn were probably a clarification of the two words before
> them in the previous question, but it was still not interpretable.

At an earlier age she often tried to repeat what Fred had said. In the following
instance, Fred (5;9) had been told not to polish the soles of his shoes, and he
had said, "All right. I'll wipe that off. That can be easily removed." And
Leslie repeated,

> /E E r/   'easily removed'   (2;4)

This same recency effect, that of producing the final portion of an utterance

Table 8-1
Age of Acquisition of Question Words

Child[a]	Where Sem[b]	Where Lex[c]	What Sem	What Lex	Who Sem	Who Lex	Why Sem	Why Lex	How Sem	How Lex	When Sem	When Lex	Which Sem	Which Lex
Leslie	2;10	3;7	3;2	3;7	4;1		3;0	3;6		4;1				4;1
Adam		2;4		2;4		2;4		3;2		2;4				3;2
Eve		1;7		1;7				1;7		2;2		2;2		
Sarah	2;5	2;5	2;5	3;0		3;0		3;8		3;8				3;8
Hildegard		1;11		2;1		2;5		1;10		2;4		2;6		
K	1;10	2;4		2;7		2;5		2;9						2;4
Christy		2;1		2;1										
Rina		2;1												
Seppo		2;2												

[a]Data on Adam, Eve, and Sarah from Ursula Bellugi, "The development of interrogative structures in children's speech," *The Development of Language Functions*, edited by K.F. Riege (Ann Arbor: University of Michigan Center for Human Growth and Development, Report No. 8, 1965); Hildegard from Werner F. Leopold, *Speech Development of a Bilingual Child*, 4 vols. (Evanston, Ill.: Northwestern University Press, 1939-1949); K from M.M. Lewis, *Infant Speech, A Study of the Beginnings of Language* (New York: Humanities Press, 1951); Christy from Wick Miller and Susan M. Ervin, "The development of grammar in child language," *The Acquisition of Language*, edited by Ursula Bellugi and Roger Brown, Monographs of the Society for Research in Child Development, Vol. 29, No. 7, 1964; and Rina and Seppo from Melissa Bowerman, *Early Syntactic Development* (London: Cambridge University Press, 1973).

[b]Semantic use: the question was interpreted as meaning the question word being considered, e.g.,

Sarah: at?   'What is that?'

[c]Lexical use: the lexical item was used though not necessarily adult phonological form, e.g.,

K: /veəz ə king/?   'Where's the string?'

one has heard, may also apply to original utterances. While there is nothing of a fixed-final-position nature in questions in English that compares with the invariant initial position of the *wh* question words, there are classes of words that naturally fall at the end of a question as opposed to the beginning of it. Leslie tends to use only these final-position words in questions, as indicated below in the section on yes/no questions.

Regarding the data from which table 8-1 is compiled, it should be noted that there is a difference in the way age of acquisition is reported in different studies. Leopold, for example, wrote a daily diary of Hildegard's speech development.[14] His study is the most apt to record the exact age that a form is used appropriately. The Harvard study[15] and the Miller and Ervin study[16] used periods, or stages, of development, and the mean age for any given period is the one used when citing ages of these children. In the case of the other children included in the table, the age when the form was first noted is the one given, but since daily records were not taken, the form may have occurred somewhat earlier than reported.

Where and When Questions

Where and *What* are the first two question words to be acquired by most children, and *where* is usually reported to be the most frequently used. We have found very few *where* questions in Leslie's speech. Semantically, her first use of it was at 2;10:

/E/ mommy bear go? 'Where did the mommy bear go?' (2;10)

/E/ king go? 'Where did the king go? (3;0)

/E/ more bed goes? 'Where does the other bed go?' (3;2)

With the noun phrase specified and the verb specified as *go*, appropriate question words are somewhat limited, and the context in these three instances made it very clear that *where* was intended.

Extending over a period of time to almost 4;0, Leslie often avoided asking *where* questions by rephrasing her question to make it a yes/no question. For example, at 3;2 her mother said, 'We're going bye bye now.' Instead of saying "Where are we going?" Leslie made a guess, "Gwama's house?" Her mother answered, "No, to the store." This got the desired results, and the yes/no question was seldom misunderstood even though it was incomplete by adult standards. It relied on rising intonation for the question marker. At 3;2 the best Leslie could have done on a *where* question, based on the few questions she had produced, would have been to ask /E wE gO/? 'where we go?' and the possibility of this being misunderstood was far greater than the possibility that "Gwama's house?" would be misunderstood.

It may be noted from table 8-1 that Leslie has never used the word *when* as a question marker during any recording session throughout the course of the research. She used it as an adverbial conjunction at 4;0 and later, e.g.,

When I was a baby, uh, I was in my crib. . . (4;1)

She was also able to discuss future time with adverbial phrases such as:

I'm having my lunch after you finish this taping.   (3;7)

However, in discussions regarding plans, such as when the investigator would say "Maybe we'll go to the park," instead of asking "When?" which seems simple enough syntactically, she always guessed, "Now?" or "After lunch?" or some other time, requiring a yes/no answer. She knew that if the answer was *no*, the time of going to the park would be volunteered. The results were essentially the same as if she had asked "When?"

This was a strategy Leslie used many times—changing the question type to the one kind of question she handled best, the question that made use of intonation rather than lexicon and syntactic structure.

At 3;7 Leslie was first noted using *where* in its adult form, but was having difficulty formulating the sentence structure:

Look at the light. I wish I get that light down. Where its turn. . . Where its get off?   (3;7)   The investigator wasn't paying close enough attention to understand what she meant, and said "Hmmm?" Leslie repeated,

Wheres its get off?   That light off?   (3;7)

Verbal auxiliaries seem to be more of a problem for Leslie than for most children. We see here that she was still using the normal, unmarked order, but with the *where* preposed (called "preposing weak" by Brown[17]). The *s* on both *where* and *it* in the second sentence above may be an attempt to include an auxiliary. Leslie had been using *do* as a main verb at least since 2;0, but did not start using *do* as an auxiliary verb until about 4;0.

It is interesting to note that as an auxiliary, *does* was always pronounced /duz/, but as a main verb, was usually pronounced /dUəz/, e.g.,

Does this work any more?   (4;1)

See like Fred /dUəz/?   (4;1)

The lexical change that Leslie made in the first *where* question above is also interesting. She said *turn* and then corrected herself to *get*. She had used *turn* as in "My turn!" frequently, and had no doubt heard it used also as in *turn off the light*, but when she said it herself, it may not have sounded right to her. Whatever her reason, her change of lexicon made her question more difficult to understand.

The earliest examples of Leslie's using *where* questions that were completely adult in syntax were at 4;7:

Where is it coming from? (4;7)

And the brother said, "Where's your breakfast, Baby?" (4;7)

What Questions

Many diaries and child language studies report that young children use some form of "What's that?" frequently and at early ages. Brown says that Adam, Eve, and Sarah said "What dat?" hundreds of times during Stages I and II; "it was their most frequent question."[18] It was a favorite question also for Fred, John, and Gregory, but not for Leslie.

This question can have two similar meanings: What is the nature or function of that object, or What is that object called? Leopold, for example, remarks that Hildegard used practically no naming questions at all of the type "What do you call this?"[19] Hildegard did use "What's that?" in asking for more general kinds of information.

While Leslie did not ask "What's that?" (in that form) until she was past 4;1, she had several questions that were semantically equivalent to the two meanings just mentioned for "What's that?":

/*th*ith/? 'What's this?' (3;0) Pointing to a caterpillar.

/E *th*at/? 'What's that?' (3;0) She thought she heard a noise upstairs and was asking about it.

What is these are? (3;9)

/E *th*Ez ko/? 'What are these called?' (3;2) This was her usual request for a lexical item.

/gEkIn *th*ath/? 'This kind was?' or 'What is this?' (3;0) She was pointing to the earrings the investigator was wearing and wanted a name for them.

While Leslie seldom asked "What's that?" she enjoyed having others ask her that question. She enjoyed naming things—practicing her repertoire of words—especially between about 2;5 and 2;10. She enjoyed it the most when she played the game in her own room where virtually all the objects were familiar to her, but she had difficulty in introducing the game. Her most frequent method was to go to an object, point to it and name it, then look expectantly at the investigator, hoping to be asked to name something else. Others have commented on children's pleasure in naming objects at certain ages. It is the game of "What's that?" in reverse.

No questions that could be interpreted as *what* questions were asked during recording sessions before the age of 3;2. Leslie's early *what* questions (3;2 to 3;7) were formulated in the two ways the "What's that?" questions were formed: either they had no semblance of a question word, or the question word was represented by /E/:

Daddy doing?   'What is Daddy doing?'   (3;2)

/E/ s-t-e-r-e-o spell?   'What do these letters spell?'   (3;2)

/E/ he doing?   'What's he doing?'   (3;2)

/E tAk E/ shoes off for?   'What did you take your shoes off for?'   (3;2)

In the discussion of Leslie's use of /E/~/A/ as a functor in Chapter 5, we were unable to discover Leslie's rule for determining which of these two vowels she would use in any given instance. However, as the first element in a question, she almost always used /E/. The possibility remains that Leslie may not have had a question word, such as *what* or *where*, in mind in using this /E/ in initial position in these questions since she very frequently used an /E/ or /A/ with other kinds of questions as well as in initial position in sentences other than questions (see Chapter 5).

Later questions using the lexical item *what* follow:

What my teacher name?   (3;7)

We saw. . .what call on with a red. . .suit?   (3;11) The investigator asked "Hmmm?" and she said,

Somebody told us that guy with the red suit.   (3;11)

Fred said "Red Riding Hood!" Leslie agreed. They had been to a bakery and had seen a birthday cake decorated with the story of Red Riding Hood.

What he did over here? (4;7)

What /kIn ə / color eyes I got? (4;2)

And one guy said, "Hey, what is this lotion doing?" (4;7)

The questions, "What is these are?" and "Wheres its get off?" may be indications of Leslie's awareness of the necessity for some auxiliary following the questions word: *Is these are* does not follow normal word order, though her change does not follow the usual transformation. On the other hand, we noted earlier that question words are usually learned easily because of their initial position in the sentence. If Leslie is learning patterns according to position in the sentence, she may have noticed that *is* frequently follows *what* and *where*. She may think of *what is* as a unit of some sort.

While most examples by 4;7 are close to adult syntax, including the auxiliary *do*, "What he did over here?" is an exception. It is an example of what Brown calls a "preposed strong" question because it includes an inflected verb along with the preposed question words.[20]

Who Questions

As may be seen from table 8-1, most children used *where, what,* and *who* before *why, how,* and *when.* Only one instance of Leslie's use of *whose,* which may have been an attempt to produce *who*, has been recorded. Leslie had been giving names that started with the letter J. The investigator was prompting her to also give the name of one of her best friends, a boy named Jason, whom she called /vEzəntz/ or some variation of this. The investigator said "And you know another one, too. You know a little boy, he's about your size."

Whose is it? (4;1)

She may have meant "Whose name?" but it is more likely that she wanted to say "Who is it?" and she was adding the sibilant here just as she had to the *where* and *what*, mentioned above. (Incidentally, Leslie was surprised that *Jason* started with a *j*, though she had listed *John, Jack, Jill,* and other *j* words. She did not seem to have analyzed the initial sound of Jason as a *j*. We assume she had analyzed it as a *v*.)

It would appear that some *wh* questions are semantically more important to some children than others. In Stage III, for example, Sarah and Adam each produced two *who* questions apiece, fewer than *where* or *what* questions, and Eve had not started using *who* yet. Even if *who* is within a child's phonological productive competence, there may be fewer occasions for caring about using it.

Why, How Come, and How Questions

Whereas Fred had badgered his mother with hundreds of *why* questions, Leslie was recorded using only four of them. The first question of Leslie's that was interpreted as a why-question appeared at 3;0:

/A/ got this noise on?   'Why is there a noise?'   (3;0)

Later utterances using the lexical item *why* follow:

Why you have a nose?   (3;6)

Why you got all black telephones?   (3;7)

You give me a spoon.   Why?   (3;11)

The *why* is preposed in the first two, but not in the third; otherwise these three sentences are the same in having maintained normal word order. No transformations have taken place.

Beginning at 3;7 and continuing until the end of this study, Leslie used *how come*? to ask questions that are semantically the same as why-questions. A look at the acceptability of the normal sentence structure with *how come* suggests a reason for this strategy:

How come /E A krisə/ time here?   'How come it's Christmas time here?'   (3;7) It was September and the building across the street had Christmas lights burning along the eaves. The investigator, however, had not noticed the lights and was puzzled by the question. She asked, "Hmmm? It's Christmas time?"   Leslie answered, "No. I ist teasing."   It was preferable for her to close the subject rather than try to explain her question.

How come this guy has a red face?   (4;7)

How come you're sitting there?   (4;7)

How come they're not?   (4;7)

How come this guy is smiling?   (4;7)

When *how come* is substituted for *why*, the question does not need a transformation—the normal sentence pattern is correct. The question becomes an embedded clause, e.g., "How does it happen that _____ ?"

Only three questions using just *how* were noted:

How is he doing it?   (4;7)

How do you know I were was?   'How do you know where I
   was?'   (4;7)   *Were* was not phonetically very distinct, and
   she may have intended to be saying *where*, in which case the
   word order would still be wrong.

How do you be on the train for?   'Why do you go on a
   train?'   (4;7)

As the gloss suggests, *how* was not the appropriate lexical choice for her meaning in the last example. No way comes to mind for expressing her assumed
meaning if one starts with *how*.

As can be seen from these examples, Leslie's early lack of the lexical items
referred to here as questions words represents only a part of Leslie's difficulty.
It should be pointed out that soon after 2;0 she had other words in her lexicon
with initial *h* and *w* even though she didn't at that time have *hw*. However, it
is usual for children to use the simple *w* in initial position in *where, what, when*,
etc. Leslie's problem was not just a lack of lexical items appropriate for questions. Her more serious problem was her inability to transform the normal
sentence order to appropriate order for questions.

Yes/No Questions

The bulk of Leslie's questions were of the type that required a yes or no
answer. It has been assumed that she preferred this type of question because
it uses a rising intonation, offering a reliable mark of a question. Her *wh*
questions did not have this advantage and were more often misunderstood than
yes/no questions. However, even for these questions at early ages, the listener
was forced to rely rather heavily on the context of the situation to interpret
Leslie's questions.

Questions from about 2;9 to 3;0 follow certain patterns, as may be noted
from the *underlined* words in the questions below. Lexical items that are in
final position in the adult form of Leslie's questions (her assumed meanings)
are those she produced. These lexical items and their sentence positions are:
subject, verb, object (direct and/or indirect) and adverb. Any one, two, three
or four of these may be present, but they must be in the order just given.

In initial position in the question is an /E/, or in some cases, nothing:

$$Q \rightarrow \left\{ \begin{array}{c} /E/ \\ \emptyset \end{array} \right\} + \left\{ \begin{array}{c} S \\ \emptyset \end{array} \right\} + \left\{ \begin{array}{c} V \\ \emptyset \end{array} \right\} + \left\{ \begin{array}{c} O \\ \emptyset \end{array} \right\} + \left\{ \begin{array}{c} Adv \\ \emptyset \end{array} \right\} .$$

$$\quad\quad\quad 1 \quad\quad 2 \quad\quad 3 \quad\quad 4 \quad\quad 5$$

/E *mE*/? 'Is it for *me*?' (A call on her toy telephone.)

/E *mI br*/? 'Will you read *my book*?'

/di *wE mIn*/? 'Will you *read mine*?'

/ə *dadE*/? 'Is that *a daddy*?'

/E *gEkI mE*/? 'Will you ring the *phone* for *me*?'

/E *beth gOing*/? 'Is the *bus going*?'

/E *tAk EkI aut*/? 'Can you *take this kind out*?' (This kind = a pencil that was stuck in a truck.)

/tA *par nau*/? 'Shall I *take* the puzzle *apart now*?' Leslie put her hand on the puzzle, making her meaning clear, so it was unnecessary for her to use her multi-purpose *gi kine* to refer to the puzzle.

/E *gEkIn on*/? 'Is the *tape recorder on*?'

/E *han wA*/? 'Will you move your *hand away*?' This might have been considered an imperative except for the rising intonation.

/əga/? 'Shall I do it *again*?'

/E *wUthtr*/? 'Is that a *rooster*?'

/E *an E her*/? 'Would you keep your *hand in here*?' (to prevent the page from turning)

/gEkIn wIr/? 'Is *this kind water*?'

/E *gEkIn fath*/? 'Is the *tape recorder* running too *fast*?'

/A *gEkIn kwOth*/? 'Would you *close* the *purse*?'

The last question presents an exception to our stated rule about the ordering within a sentence as well as different initial vowel. Here we have $Q \rightarrow /A/ + O + V$. It is possible that her meaning was "I want the purse closed," though she did use rising intonation.

Of the twelve possible sentence orderings offered by our rule above (S, V, O, Adv, S+V, S+O, S+O+Adv, S+Adv, V+O, V+O+Adv, V+Adv, O+Adv), the only sentence types that were not found in our sample were

$$Q \rightarrow \left\{ \begin{array}{c} /E/ \\ \emptyset \end{array} \right\} + V, \text{ and } Q \rightarrow \left\{ \begin{array}{c} /E/ \\ \emptyset \end{array} \right\} + S + O + Adv.$$

As mentioned above, Leslie did not ask many questions, and these omissions may have been by chance.

In examining the *wh* questions discussed earlier, we note that they fit this exact pattern syntactically at this age up through about 3;3. Leslie started using yes/no questions at an earlier age than the *wh* questions. The only distinguishing feature in the production of these two kinds of questions at this age was the intonation pattern. From the listener's point of view, the interpretation of some as *wh* questions and others as yes/no questions was compelling, not from the syntax of the question, but from the intended meaning as indicated by the total context of the situation, and by Leslie's reaction to replies.

Later Yes/No Questions

Leslie's advancement with question transformations was slow compared to the Harvard children, Hildegard, Fred, and other children with whom she has been compared. Her meanings were not immature by comparison, but her syntax was:

Read this? 'Will you read this?' (3;1)

I am? 'Do you know who (or what) I am?' (when she's pretending to be someone else) (3;4)

You want one? (3;4)

I like to do in swimming pool? 'Do you know what I like to do in the swimming pool?' (3;5)

/I yIk/?   'Do you know what I like?'   (3;6)

See this hat?   (3;7)

You go with me?   (3;7)

Yeah, know whats is it?   (4;1)

Does this write?   (4;1)

A word that start with K?   (4;1)   'Do you know another word
   that starts with K?'   This was not a question for information.
   She wanted to tell the word she knew.

See what I mading?   (4;2)

Do it hurt when you scratch it?   (4;2)

Want to see how it flies?   (4;2)

Can you crack this open?   (4;4)

Can you hold this right here?   (4;4)

Does Fred have it of his class?   (5;2)   'Does Fred have one in
   his classroom?'

Discussion

With questions, as with negation and other aspects of Leslie's speech development, it can be seen that it was in the earliest stages that she could most
accurately be described as 'slow.' By the time she was 4;0 the kinds of syntactic
immaturities we find in her questions do not usually deter the listener from
understanding her.   By this time there were relatively few instances in which she
was asked to repeat or rephrase her question.   Even though there is abundant
evidence that she is learning the syntax and is constantly changing her own rules
in an effort to come closer to the adult model, there is little evidence that she is
aware of this process, in contrast to her awareness of her phonological and lexical
difficulties, as discussed in Chapters 4 and 5.

Notes

1. D. Morehead, and D. Ingram, "The development of base syntax in normal and linguistically deviant children," *Papers and Reports on Child Language Development,* Committee on Linguistics, Stanford University, 1970.
2. Jon Eisenson, *Aphasia in Children* (New York: Harper and Row, 1972).
3. M.A.K. Halliday, "Relevant models of language," *Explorations in the functions of language* (London: Edward Arnold, 1973).
4. Ursula Bellugi, "The development of interrogative structures in children's speech," in *The development of language functions,* edited by K.F. Riege (Ann Arbor: University of Michigan Center for Human Growth and Development, Report No. 8, 1965), pp. 103-137.
5. Melissa Bowerman, *Early syntactic development* (London: Cambridge University Press, 1973).
6. Roger Brown, "The development of *wh* questions in child speech," *Journal of Verbal Learning and Verbal Behavior* 7 (1968):279-90.
7. Roger Brown, Courtney Cazden, and Ursula Bellugi-Klima, "The child's grammar from I to III," in *Minnesota Symposia on Child Psychology,* vol. II, edited by J.P. Hill (Minneapolis: University of Minnesota Press, 1968), pp. 28-73.
8. Jeffrey S. Gruber, "Topicalization in child language," *Foundations of language* 3 (1967):37-65.
9. E.S. Klima, and Ursula Bellugi, "Syntactic regularities in the speech of children," in *Psycholinguistic papers,* edited by J. Lyons and R.J. Wales (Edinburgh, Scotland: Edinburgh University Press, 1966), pp. 183-208.
10. Werner F. Leopold, *Speech development of a bilingual child,* vol. 4 (Evanston, Ill.: Northwestern University Press, 1949).
11. Wick Miller, and Susan M. Ervin, "The development of grammar in child language," in *The acquisition of language,* edited by Ursula Bellugi and Roger Brown, Monographs of the Society for Research in Child Development, Vol. 29, No. 1, 1964, pp. 9-34.
12. Susan M. Ervin-Tripp, "Some strategies for the first two years," *Language acquisition and communicative choice: Essays by Susan Ervin-Tripp,* edited by Anwar S. Dil (Stanford, Calif.: Stanford University Press, 1973), pp. 216-17.
13. Ibid., p. 213.
14. Werner F. Leopold, *Speech development of a bilingual child,* vol. 4 (Evanston, Ill.: Northwestern University Press, 1949).
15. Bellugi, "The development of interrogative structures in children's speech."
16. Miller, and Ervin, "The development of grammar in child language."
17. Brown, "The development of *wh* questions in child speech."
18. Ibid., p. 283.
19. Leopold, *Speech development of a bilingual child,* vol. 3, 1949, p. 68.
20. Brown, "The Development of *wh* questions in child speech."

9 Conclusions

Why do some children acquire language slowly and with apparent difficulty? This is the question we would like to be able to answer but cannot. We do not doubt that there are answers, but the problem is extremely complex and a great deal of research must be done before conclusive answers can be offered.

We have, however, been able to draw some conclusions regarding the speech development of one child, Leslie. She is an unusually bright child whose speech development was very slow, particularly at early stages. She does not represent *all* slow speech developers, but it seems certain that there are many other children who are much like her. Some of the conclusions we draw here may be suggestive regarding the slow speech development of these other slow, but bright, speech developers who are like Leslie.

In Chapter 1 it was stated that the objectives of this study were to: (1) describe Leslie's speech development, (2) compare her development to that of other children, (3) look for causal factors for her slowness in speech acquisition, and (4) examine the educational implications of our findings. Each of these objectives and the questions asked in relation to them will be considered here.

Descriptive Aspects

Chapters 2 through 8 not only describe Leslie's linguistic development, but provide information about many characteristics she possesses that may bear on her linguistic development. This is done on the assumption that language development is closely related to many other aspects of a child's development and to his total environment. For example, we have seen that Leslie is a child who is accomplished on roller skates and on a jungle jim, who works puzzles easily, and who sculps nicely. She is better at doing things than talking about them. These characteristics are recorded here, in part for the benefit of future research, and in part to help explain Leslie's intellectual abilities, as discussed in Chapter 3.

One of the questions we asked at the beginning of our research was whether or not all aspects of Leslie's speech development would be slow. At that point, her slowness with the phonological aspects was all that was readily apparent, and it was thought that a child might be quite slow in this way and yet keep pace with other children in the development of syntax, morphology, lexicon, etc. We have concluded that it was only the semantic and paralinguistic aspects of Leslie's speech that were not slow in developing, while the phonological, morphological, syntactic, and lexical aspects of speech production were slow.

It is stressed here that it is speech *production* that is slow. There is ample evidence that Leslie was comprehending language. For example, while Leslie repeatedly had difficulty in producing words she needed to express her meanings and relied heavily on multi-purpose words, her passive vocabulary was in the 99th percentile, as evidenced by her score on the Peabody Picture Vocabulary Test (see Chapter 3). She understood words when she heard them even though she could not recall them for use when she wanted them. We saw that Leslie was very slow in producing functors, but there was no evidence that she failed to understand their use in speech directed to her.

We have seen repeatedly that Leslie was absorbing the meaning of language, was reorganizing what she heard and storing the meaning in long-term memory even though she was not analyzing it in ways that would make it possible for her to reproduce it in the form in which she received it. We find it necessary to stress this lack of a relationship between retarded speech development and retarded mental development because it is so often thought that there is a correlation, that the child who is slow in expressing ideas verbally, such as Leslie, has fewer ideas to express—is simply less bright—than the child who learns to express ideas verbally at a very early age, such as Fred.

Tests given to Leslie during the last half of her fifth year indicate her mental development was advanced for her age (I.Q., 139); she is unquestionably bright (see Chapter 3).

It is interesting to note that Leslie's processing of nonspeech sounds did not offer the difficulty that speech sounds did. She learned melodies easily, learned intonation patterns easily, and mimicked nonspeech sounds, as discussed in Chapter 1. While language is primarily localized in the left hemisphere of the brain, the learning of melodies and intonation contours is located in the right hemisphere. Critchley also suggests the importance of the right hemisphere in creative literary work.[1] We have suggested that Leslie used language creatively, and theories of brain dominance offer a partial explanation for this apparent dichotomy of creative use of language in the presence of slow speech development.

Comparative Aspects

When we look at the comparison of Leslie's speech development with that of other children, we do not find that the order of acquisition of certain elements of speech was very different from that of other children. If anything was acquired in an order different than the usual pattern, it was phonemes. In a summary of the order in which the sounds of the language are acquired Ervin-Tripp says, "If two consonants are alike in manner of articulation, one will be labial, the other dental or alveolar (e.g., /p/ versus /t/), resulting in the common lack of /k/."[2] Her generalizations are consistent with Jakobson's predictions about the order of acquisition of the sound system by children.[3] As may be seen in Chapter 4, Leslie, age 0;11, had three places of articulation among her first five monoremes: labial /m/ and /b/, dental /d/, and velar /g/. Whereas some children are said to acquire a velar in prespeech sounds[4] and lose them when speech begins, Leslie maintained the velar as a permanent part of her phonemic inventory from this first speech stage on. If this order of acquisition is truly different from that of most other children, it may account for Leslie's greater difficulty with the phonological system: it may be more efficient to start out with only two contrasting consonants instead of three. It must be borne in mind, however, that the generalizations of both Jakobson and Ervin-Tripp are made on the phonological studies of a comparatively small number of children and Leslie's case may not be as unusual as it appears.

In any event, Leslie was not slow in acquiring the first set of phonemes of English. She acquired at least as many (perhaps one more) at about the same age as other children, but progressed more slowly in completing the task than other children with whom she was compared. She started using monoremes at approximately the same age that other children do, and produced progressively longer and more complex sentences as she became older, just as other children do, but by the time she was past four, her sentences were longer and more complex, at the same time that they contained more immaturities than those of other children. The complexity of the sentences, we assume, is a function of the complexity of the ideas she wished to express—a function of her intelligence—while the immaturities are a result of her slow speech development. She omitted functors just as all children do at earliest stages of speech development, but continued for a longer period of time without them than most children do. She used a great deal of reduplication and consonant harmony. All children use at least some; she used more than most other children.

The most telling way in which Leslie differed from other children was in the extent of her speech immaturity and the period of time over which this continued, not in the nature of the difference itself.

We were interested in finding possible early indicators of slow speech development. While we did not hope to find anything that would predict with certainty that a child would be slow in speech development, we hoped that certain characteristics could be found that would offer clues at twelve or possibly eighteen months of age as to whether a child should be watched for further indications of slow speech development. Because of the paucity of recent studies by linguists of children with slow speech development, we find it impossible to make any generalizations about predictors of slow speech development. Many long-term longitudinal studies need to be done before any such generalizations can be made. Based on our research with Leslie, however, we consider the following characteristics of Leslie's to be worth examining as possible predictors of slow speech development:

1. Small amount of babbling
2. Strong and continued preference for velars
3. Small amount of vocal response to verbal stimulation
4. Strong reliance on reduplicated forms in early words.

These are very early signs that *may* be predictors of slow speech development. Perhaps it would be more accurate to suggest that the slow speech developers will most likely be found among the children who exhibit the above characteristics. If a child babbled a great deal, responded when an adult spoke to him by animated babbling, as Fred did, we would be extremely surprised if he turned out to be a slow speech developer.

In Chapter 2, five ways in which Nice considered slow speech developers to be different from normal developers were itemized: (1) absence of inflection, (2) omission of minor words (functors), (3) small size of vocabulary, (4) infantile stammer, and (5) the presence of original expression.[5]

The absence of inflection, the omission of minor words, and the presence of original expression are characteristic of all children in the early stages of development. Therefore, these characteristics cannot be thought of as predictors of slow speech development, but it becomes an indication that a child *is* slow in speech development if he does not acquire the use of inflections, etc., at some age that can be considered 'average.' The study of language acquisition has not yet reached a point where standards can be set and a child can be said to fall within an 'average' range. Therefore, the use of the acquisition of inflections or functors, for example, becomes a difficult measure by which to determine whether or not a child is, in fact, a slow speech developer.

Closer inspection of these three characteristics might reveal some qualitative differences, e.g., there may be a difference in the kinds of original expression used by slow speech developers. However, if such qualitative differences exist, we have not found them.

As for the small size of vocabulary, we discussed in Chapter 2 the probable miscount of R's vocabulary by Nice inasmuch as she was looking for clearly understandable words, and the child with slow phonological development typically does not produce very many of these.

That leaves an infantile stammer as a mark of the slow speech developer, and we are not certain how this is defined. However, as commented earlier, Leslie did use more 'uh's' and other speech sounds while pausing during speech than Fred did. Ordinarily the listener tends to ignore these to a large extent, both in children and adults. In transcribing Leslie's speech, many such sounds have not been transcribed. This may be related to fluency in speech, which will be considered under the category of educational implications below.

Leslie's strategies for language acquisition

There were a certain number of strategies that Leslie used that seemed to be somewhat different, or more extreme, than the strategies used by most children in language acquisition. They are briefly stated here.

1. She relied heavily on words of reduplicated-syllable form. At earliest ages, both vowels and consonants were reduplicated. Later, only the consonant was reduplicated. (See Chapter 4.)
2. Syllables, whether reduplicated or not, rarely were VC in form at early ages. (See Chapter 4.)
3. Vowels were used extensively without consonants to represent morphemes or words. (See Chapter 4.)
4. Leslie appeared to be conscious of her phonological difficulties and drilled herself on difficult sound patterns, such as adding a final voiceless velar to words, or drilled herself on particular words that were difficult for her, such as *box*. (See Chapter 4.)
5. She relied on multi-purpose words to substitute for lexical items she didn't know, couldn't recall, had been unable to analyze phonetically, or was unable to produce. (See Chapter 5.)
6. She relied on simple fixed-form utterances such as her "Watch-me!" construction and "Know-what?" questions. Once mastered, these syntactic structures could be used efficiently with little change in lexicon. (See Chapter 6.)
7. She relied heavily on paralinguistic features, such as intonation patterns and gestures, to mark negation, interrogation, and other meanings in language that were difficult for her to express structurally. Questions which the listener would expect to be *wh* questions were frequently structured as yes/no questions, which rely on rising intonation patterns. (See Chapters 7 and 8.)

While these strategies are not necessarily unique among the children Leslie was compared with, Fred, for example, used none of these strategies, and it appears that children for whom speech production is easy do not find it necessary to employ such measures.

Causal Factors

Slobin points out that "Because we communicate through the rapidly-fading, temporally-ordered auditory modality, we must have strategies for quickly programming and decipering messages."[6] It is somewhere in this quick programming of the auditory message that Leslie is unable to perform as well as most children. She deciphers the message for meaning, but she does not seem to analyze language phonologically so she can reproduce it in the same form in which she heard it. Slobin goes on to say "The constraints on linguistic performance are both short-term and long-term. The short-term have to do with the ongoing use of speech, and the long-term with the storage and organization of the linguistic system." It is in the area of the short-term processing that Leslie appeared to have difficulty, as was pointed up in her performance on the Stanford-Binet Intelligence Scale (see Chapter 3). As was mentioned in Chapter 1, Ervin-Tripp lists five necessary components for a child's Language Acquisition System (LAS).[7] The first of these is "Selective retention of features in short term memory, particularly including order of acoustic input." Leslie was, of course, not completely lacking in this skill, but it appeared that she performed much more poorly in this respect than in other aspects of language acquisition. At early ages, material presented verbally was processed for meaning much more efficiently than it was processed for reproduction.

After Leslie started to learn to read, there were certain situations in which it appeared that Leslie analyzed written language, stored it more efficiently for reproduction—both written and spoken reproduction—than she did spoken language. For example, after reading a word, she seemed to pronounce it more accurately than after hearing it pronounced carefully. She also remembered how to spell it after seeing it written, whereas she didn't necessarily remember how to pronounce a word after hearing it. Leslie was a good speller, usually spelling correctly words she had seen. By 5;0 she could hold her own in a game of Scrabble with other family members. She also followed written directions more easily than verbal directions. Her teachers at school considered this to be a factor in placing her in the first grade class where many instructions are written, rather than putting her in kindergarten where instructions are all verbal.

It appears that second-language learning requires many of the same skills that first-language acquisition requires. Pimsleur, Sundland, and McIntyre, in a comprehensive study of the problems of underachievers in foreign language learning among students who are achievers in other areas of study, found that "under-achievers did not perform less well than average-achievers in tests of verbal intelligence (*Vocabulary*), verbal reasoning (*Linguistic Analysis*) or word fluency (*Rhymes*), but they did so on the two tests of auditory ability. Such a finding appears to indicate that the so-called 'talent for languages' resides principally in the domain of auditory ability, which may be described as the ability to receive and process information through the ear."[8]

Carroll reports similar results from a large body of research conducted during World War II in an effort to select for foreign language study only those individuals who were most likely to succeed.[9] Among the many findings he discusses are that facility in learning to understand and speak a foreign language depends on traits that are independent of intelligence per se (just as Pimsleur et al. found). Rather, it is a special "group of talents" that are required. Carroll also concluded more specifically that "One of the most important abilities required in learning a foreign language is the *ability to 'code' auditory phonetic material* in such a way that this material can be recognized, identified, and remembered over something longer than a few seconds." To illustrate something of the cognitive nature of the coding task, Carroll tells of a woman who had received a low score on the Phonetic Script Test. She was asked to listen to two nonsense syllables, /thAj/ and /thaj/, then spend ten seconds performing mental arithmetic, then repeat the two syllables. This is a simple task for most people, but this woman was unable to do it under these conditions, although she could repeat the two syllables immediately after she heard them. Carroll concludes that it is "not the ability to make an echoic response to phonetic material, but the ability somehow to 'code' or represent it in imagery so that it can be recognized and reproduced after an intervening period filled with other activity."

The underachiever in second-language learning appears to have many of Leslie's characteristics. As has been pointed out, this auditory ability necessary for first- or second-language learning is a rather specialized ability that is unrelated to intelligence, but it would appear that the child who is lacking in it is far more disadvantaged in our school systems than the disability would warrant. Furthermore, a child such as Leslie may tend to lose confidence in himself before reaching school age as it becomes apparent to him and to his family that he is failing in an important task—language learning. Special effort needs to be made to reassure the child of his overall capabilities.

Educational Implications

Nice concluded her study of the slow speech development of her daughter, R, by saying that a child learns to talk when he needs to, and "most children learn through imitation to speak earlier than they really need to."[10] It is not clear just what Nice meant by *need*, but one cannot listen to a child such as Leslie struggle with language, watch her frustration at not being understood, and think she is just waiting to use the adult system at some time in the future when she "needs to." A child needs language from a very early age on, but there is never a time or place when a child needs skill with language more than in the educational system in this country. Verbal skills of very particular kinds are highly prized in schools, and it seems appropriate for linguists to look for ways of helping preschool children acquire these skills.

It was hoped that the strategies that Leslie used in maximizing her own speech development might suggest to us some means for helping other children who were not so aware of their difficulties, or who did not work so assiduously at the task of language acquisition as Leslie did. It appears, however, that the strategies that Leslie used—the self-drilling on words and sounds that were hard for her, etc., need to be self-motivated in order to be useful at these early ages. If someone else had said to Leslie, "Today I want you to practice saying *dress*," the effect would almost certainly have been adverse. However, the effect on Leslie of knowing that individuals such as her family and the investigator were interested in her speech development may have given her some of the motivation to work on her language harder than she might have otherwise. Parents usually consider it to be kinder to ignore the child's immaturities in language. This may not be the most beneficial attitude, particularly where phonology and lexicon are concerned.

We were interested to note that Leslie appeared to be much like the Yakima Indian children we have worked with in respect to the way she programmed her own language drills and directed many of her own activities. In Chapter 2 we discussed Leslie's inability to cope in a highly structured classroom situation. We have observed the same reaction on the part of Yakima children in lower grades in public schools, whereas in the Head Start program where Yakima men and women maintain a relaxed setting, more like their own homes, the Yakima children are self-disciplined in starting and completing tasks of their own choosing, and follow nicely such instructions as "It's time to put away the toys and have your afternoon snack." They also perform creatively in story-telling and similar verbal tasks when they are in this friendly, permissive atmosphere, but react adversely to a highly structured situation without opportunity for working on their own initiative.

In a study involving the Indian children on the Warm Springs Indian Reservation, Philips also came to the conclusion that the structure of the classroom needs to be changed to take into account the fact that the sociolinguistic rules of the Indian children differ from those of the non-Indian children.[11] For example, situations in which the child was required to speak when the entire class was listening, such as having to answer questions in front of everyone and participate in "sharing time" needed to be minimized and opportunities to ask and answer questions with the teacher at her desk without an audience, and working in small groups rather than with the entire class, etc., needed to be maximized.

It appears that Leslie is not only capable of working things out for herself, of discovering answers to questions she cannot ask, but needs to do this. The same may be true of the Yakima children.

We discussed earlier the importance of fluency in the classroom because of its effect on teachers (see Chapter 1). Leslie would certainly have to be called non-fluent as an early speaker, but we have seen the many ways that she has caught up, or nearly so, and we hesitate to predict whether or not she will be a fluent speaker as an adult. We do not hesitate to predict that Fred will be, but Leslie is not likely to attain the mastery of language that Fred is likely to. However, she may be what is considered fluent without that degree of mastery. Carroll discusses three kinds of fluency and ways of measuring them: (1) ideational fluency, which measures an individual's facility in calling up as many ideas as possible about a given topic or theme in which the number of different ideas, rather than their quality is at issue; (2) word fluency, which concerns an individual's facility in thinking of words with certain formal characteristics, such as those that begin with a certain letter when spelled; and (3) fluency of expression, which represents the individual's facility in formulating ideas—putting them in grammatically acceptable words and constructions.[12]

Carroll says

> There has been relatively little research on the possible heredi-
> tary etiology of those aspects of language ability that are largely
> independent of intelligence. We have some evidence of a genetic
> basis for the special difficulties that a certain small percentage of
> children, particularly males, have with beginning reading and spell-
> ing, and later, with foreign languages, even though the children may
> be otherwise quite intelligent. This syndrome is called *specific
> language disability* and is characterized by difficulty in encoding
> and storing auditory (phonetic) information and tying it with
> visual symbols. It may have a close relation to the word fluency
> factor mentioned earlier.[13]

We have compared Leslie's history with that of several children who were being helped by speech pathologists for just such disabilities—essentially, the failure to be able to learn to read. On the surface, the similarities in speech development between these children and Leslie are striking, right up to the point of being able to read. The most likely explanation that comes to mind for this difference was in Leslie's learning to read almost as early as she learned to talk, i.e., around 2;0 she began to learn the sounds and shapes of the letters of the alphabet, the first task in learning to read. Her acquisition of verbal language was, of course, more advanced than her acquisition of written language, but whereas it is usually thought that a child has a mastery of verbal language before he begins the acquisition of reading, essentially as a second language, this was not the case with Leslie.

We have not formally tested her skill in 'word fluency,' but in games she performed well in thinking of words that started either with certain phonemes or certain graphemes, whichever way the game was presented to her. This sort of practice from age two to four seems certain to have had a favorable effect on her learning to read. As described in Chapter 2, Leslie was reading very simple stories with selected words before she was four.

This interweaving of visual and auditory language learning at a very early age may be the difference between Leslie's skill in reading and spelling and that of other children with what has been called specific language disability.

A final implication of this study was suggested above: a slow speech developer such as Leslie will not be expected to have the ability to learn to speak a second language easily. She may learn to read another language without difficulty, but measured abilities in second-language learning are almost always relative to speaking ability, not reading ability.

We believe this study has been useful in offering a description of the speech development of one child who is very bright, yet slow in producing speech. We are confident that there are many other children whose intellectual abilities and speech development are similar to Leslie's. There are undoubtedly many others who are slow in producing speech who are not so gifted intellectually. More descriptive studies of such children might make it possible to find patterns in slow speech development, pinpoint causal factors and determine courses of action most likely to prevent such children from being disadvantaged in school, and possibly throughout life.

Notes

1. M. Critchley, "Speech and speech-loss in relation to duality of the brain," in *Interhemispheric relations and cerebral dominance*, edited by V.B. Mountcastel (Baltimore: The Johns Hopkins University Press, 1962), pp. 208-213.

2. Susan M. Ervin-Tripp, "Language development," in *Review of child development research*, vol. 2, edited by L.W. Hoffman and M. L. Hoffman (New York: Russell Sage Foundation, 1966), pp. 68-69.

3. Roman Jakobson, *Child language aphasia and phonological universals* (The Hague: Mouton, 1968).

4. Ibid.

5. Margaret Nice, "A child who would not talk," *Pedagogical Seminary* 32 (1925):105-42.

6. Dan I. Slobin, "Cognitive prerequisites for the development of grammar," in *Studies of child language development*, edited by C.A. Ferguson and Dan I. Slobin (New York: Holt, Rinehart and Winston, 1973), pp. 175-208.

7. Susan M. Ervin-Tripp, "Some strategies for the first two years," in *Language acquisition and communicative choice: Essays by Susan Ervin-Tripp,* edited by Anwar S. Dil (Stanford, California: Stanford University Press, 1973), pp. 204-238.

8. Paul Pimsleur, Donald M. Sundland, and Ruth D. McIntyre, *Under-achievement in foreign language learning,* Final report to the U.S. Department of Health, Education and Welfare, Ohio State University, 1963, pp. 36-37.

9. John B. Carroll, "The prediction of success in intensive foreign language training," in *Training research and education*, edited by Robert Glaser (Pittsburgh, Pa.: University of Pittsburgh Press, 1962), pp. 87-136.

10. Nice, "A child who would not talk."

11. Susan U. Philips, "Acquisition of rules for appropriate speech usage," in *Report of the 21st annual Round Table Meeting on Linguistics and Language Studies,* edited by James E. Alatis (Washington, D.C.: Georgetown University Press, 1970), pp. 77-101.

12. John B. Carroll, *Language and thought* (Englewood Cliffs, New Jersey: Prentice-Hall, 1964).

13. Ibid., p. 69.

Glossary

Agent   The performer, or instigator, of the action identified by the verb.

Anaphoric Pronouns   Refers to a preceding word or group of words. *One* is an anaphoric pronoun in "I prefer a big bun to a little *one*." (*Do* is an anaphoric verb in "Act as we *do*.")

Aspiration   The puff of breath that accompanies the production of certain speech sounds, such as the *p* of *pin*, or *h*.

Babbling   Speech-type sounds that are made principally during the prespeech period of infancy (from perhaps six months to one year). Sometimes babbling continues after language has begun. Babbling is often interpreted as attempts at language.

Baby Talk   Speech directed to babies (or pets, etc.) by adults or older children, which is patterned according to what the adult thinks is a baby's way of speaking, or a way of speaking which adults think is appropriate for addressing young children, but which is not regarded as normal, adult use of language. This may include phonological modifications, such as *oo* for *you*, morphological modifications, such as *shoesies* for *shoes*, or lexical changes, such as *choo-choo* for *train*.

Clipped   Sounds which are produced with a greater tenseness and stronger expiration, and at a more rapid tempo than unmarked speech sounds. Vowel duration is shorter than usual and consonants tend to be voiceless.

Competence   A term brought into linguistic usage by Noam Chomsky denoting a speaker-hearer's knowledge of his language as opposed to performance, which is the actual use of language in concrete situations. The notion of competence includes a native speaker's linquistic intuitions about his language.

Consonant Harmony   A system whereby the consonants of a two-syllable word are the same, e.g., *doggie* becomes *goggie*, or at least have the same place of articulation: e.g., *coffee* becomes *koggie*, where the place of articulation (velar) is the same, though *k* is voiceless and *g* is voiced.

Content Word   A noun, verb, adjective, and some adverbs which have semantic content, as opposed to grammatical function. (See functors.)

Dental Fricative   A dental consonant is one that is produced with the tongue touching the tips of the upper teeth (*d* or *t*). A dental fricative is one produced at this same location, but with the air passage closed sufficiently to produce an audible friction, such as the initial sound in *thin* or *there*.

Dialect   The particular form of a given language that is spoken in, or originated in, a particular geographical area.

Fricatives   A consonant that is produced by narrowing of the air passages. The breath against this narrowed passage produces an audible friction as the air is expelled, as in *f, v,* or *s.* Sometimes also referred to as *spirants* or *continuants.*

Functor   A function word; one that expresses principally grammatical relationship, such as (in English) conjunctions, prepositions, auxiliaries, and suffixes such as the plural and past tense morphemes. Word classes in English may be divided into two general classes: content words and function words, or functors. (See discussion in Chapter 5.)

Grammatical Immaturities   Grammatical forms used by a child which are assumed to be a part of the child's own grammar, but do not conform to the grammar of the adults in the child's speech community, such as 'He *knowed* it,' where the child has not heard adults use the form *knowed.*

Graphemes   Letters of the alphabet.

Hearing Vocabulary   See *passive vocabulary.*

Imitation   In child language studies this term is generally used to refer to a child's repetition of an adult's sentence immediately after the adult says it, either on request or spontaneously. This is also how we are using the term.

Interrogative Reversal   The transformation of a positive statement to a question by the 'reversal' of the position of an auxiliary verb. For example, *It is red* becomes *Is it red*? or *You can play* becomes *Can you play*? by the repositioning of the auxiliary.

Language Development   As used in this study, language development refers to the internalization of the entire language system of the child's environment. This includes the paralinguistic and cultural aspects of language as well as the phonological, morphological, syntactic, and semantic aspects of language. There are not many ways of assessing a child's knowledge of his language aside from his speech behavior. In this study, therefore, reference is usually made to *speech development,* which reflects more accurately a child's *use* of his language rather than his *knowledge* of it. It is assumed that a person of any age has internalized more of his language system than he is able to express: speech development is therefore only a partial representation of language development.

Lexicon   The vocabulary or total stock of morphemes or words of a given language or of a given person.

Marked/Unmarked   The original linguistic theory of marked vs. unmarked features in phonology has been generalized to other aspects of language. In phonology oral vowels may be considered as *unmarked* while nasal vowels are *marked.* All languages have oral vowels, and they may, in addition, have nasal vowels, or they may not. No language has nasal vowels without also having oral vowels. The oral vowel, or the unmarked member of the pair oral/nasal, is the more basic. In grammar, of the pair singular/plural, the singular is the unmarked member of the pair; the plural is generally marked in English with a suffixed -s. In paralinguistics, of the pair moderate volume/ whisper, moderate volume is the unmarked member while whispering is the marked member; high pitch would be marked as opposed to moderate pitch.

Mean Length of Utterance (MLU)   The average length of a natural sequence of utterances. It is usually calculated on a basis of 50 to 100 utterances. The unit counted is the number of morphemes rather than words. The total number of morphemes is divided by the number of utterances to arrive at the MLU. (See discussion in Chapter 3.)

Medial Flap   A dental consonant in medial position in a word. It is produced by a tap of the tongue near, or against, the teethridge, as in bu*tt*er.

Mimicry   The repetition of verbal material as it was heard, including the paralinguistic features included in the original rendition, not merely a repetition of the words that were heard.

Monoreme   A one-word sentence. (See discussion in Chapter 2.)

Morpheme   The smallest individually meaningful element in a language, e.g., *clearest* consists of two morphemes—*clear* and *est* (meaning *most*) and *cats* consists of two morphemes—*cat* and *s* (meaning *more than one*, or *plural*).

Morphology   The part of grammar which studies and describes word formation; the grouping of sounds into morphemes and words, as well as compounding of words (*blackbird*), etc.

Onomatopoeic Words   Words that are imitative in origin, that reproduce the sound associated with the object, such as *moo* or *buzz*.

Orthography   The writing and spelling system of a language.

Paralinguistic   Features of language such as pitch of voice, volume, intonation patterns, and duration. Most paralinguistic features are not tied directly to a phoneme, but to some larger unit, such as a syllable, word, or phrase. Sometimes called *suprasegmental* or *prosodic* features.

Passive Vocabulary   The same as 'hearing vocabulary,' the term used by the authors of the Peabody Picture Vocabulary Test. This refers to the understanding of lexical items when they are heard, regardless of the ability to use, or produce, the words. (Words that are produced in speech are referred to as *active vocabulary*.)

Phonemes   The distinctive elementary sounds of a language, roughly corresponding to the letters of the alphabet.

Phonetics   The branch of linguistics that investigates speech sounds from a physiological, physical, and psycho-acoustical point of view. (See also *phonology*.)

Phonology   The branch of linguistics that deals with speech sounds with regard to the functions which they fulfill in the language. (See also *phonetics*.)

Pivot Word   A term used by Martin Braine to denote the small number of words in children's early two-sentences, which had a fixed position and were combined with a larger number of content words: *all* in *all broke, all dry,* and *all wet,* is a pivot word. Braine designates the content words, such as *broke, dry, wet,* as the *open* class.

Polar   Opposite in meaning. Pairs of polar adjectives are: large/small; black/white; long/short.

Productive Competence   The ability of a person to produce language as opposed to understanding it, or his knowledge about it. (See *competence.*)

Pro-word   A substitute word.

Reduplication   The repetion of an element of a syllable (or a morpheme) within the bounds of a single word, e.g., *mama* and *bye-bye* are reduplicated words.

Semantics   Related to meaning in language: the part of grammar which studies and describes the meaning of words and sentences.

Sociolinguistic Rules   Rules that determine speech behavior within a given speech community—rules that specify when one may speak, when one must remain silent, appropriate topics for the given situation, rules for changing speech style when it is directed to persons of different ages or of a different sex, etc.

Speech Development   See *language development.*

Speech Register   A variety of language based on the social situation, which functions to convey information or emotion beyond that which is conveyed by the words alone. (See discussion in Chapter 2.)

Standard Dialect   That dialect of a language which has attained literary and cultural prestige to the extent that it is accepted by the speakers of other dialects of the same language as the most 'proper' form of that language.

Syntactic Development   The aspect of language development that reflects a person's ability to put together elements (morphemes, words, phrases, clauses) to form sentences. Syntactic development starts when a child puts two words together to make a sentence.

Syntax   Sentence structure; the part of grammar which describes the relation of words to one another as parts of the structure of sentences.

Tag Questions   A short question which is added to a declarative sentence. It usually functions as a request for verification: "We're going, *aren't we*" or "He didn't do it, *did he?*" It is syntactically complex, and is sometimes replaced by a simple *Huh?* or *Right?*

Transformation   An operation on the underlying structure of a sentence to transform it into a sentence structure differing from the original sentence according to the transformational rule that was applied. A transformation may add information, rearrange information, or both. A passive transformation would change an active sentence into a passive one. A negative transformation would change a positive statement into a negative one.

Universals of Language   General principles which are true of all languages.

Unmarked   See *Marked/Unmarked*.

Utterance   A self-sufficient meaningful unit of spoken language that is preceded and followed by a pause. It may or may not be a grammatical sentence.

Velar   A consonant formed with the back of the tongue touching or near the soft palate, such as *g* or *k*.

Voiced   A consonant that is produced with a vibration of the vocal cords, such as *b*, *d*, *g*, *v*, and *z*.

Voiceless   Sounds which are produced without the vibration of the vocal cords, such as *p*, *t*, *k*, *f*, and *s*.

Index

Index

About the Author

Thelma E. Weeks received the Ph.D. in linguistics from Stanford University in 1973. Her areas of specialization are child language and sociolinguistics. She has taught at the University of California and is Director of the Center for Cross-Cultural Research, a private, nonprofit organization headquartered in Palo Alto, California.

Dr. Weeks has, for several years, been engaged in research projects concerned with language development in Yakima Indian children on the Yakima (Washington) Indian Reservation. In collaboration with her son, Dr. John R. Weeks of the Department of Sociology at San Diego State University, she has recently been engaged in a project involving measures of cognitive and linguistic skills of Yakima Indian and non-Indian children. She has also contributed to a computer-assisted reading curriculum development project at Stanford and authored the English composition sections in a series of language-arts textbooks used in elementary schools.